A Soldier's *heart*

The 3 Wars of Vietnam

Raynold A. Gauvin

 FriesenPress

One Printers Way
Altona, MB, R0G 0B0
Canada

www.friesenpress.com

This book is a memoir. It reflects the author's present recollections of experiences over time. Some events have been compressed, and some dialogue has been recreated.

The following parties for their contribution to these same maps. All were taken from www.stock.adobe.com
-The road map of the Canadian Atlantic Province of New Brunswick was by LESNEWSKI
-The political map of Maine with the Augusta was by Peter Hermes Furian
-The map of the Socialist Republic of Vietnam was by PAVALENA
-Vietnam War map from Newsweek, January 1, 1968, listing the US and enemy forces that were in Viet Nam at that time.

ISBN
978-1-03-910094-7 (Hardcover)
978-1-03-910093-0 (Paperback)
978-1-03-910095-4 (eBook)

1. HISTORY, MILITARY, VIETNAM WAR

Distributed to the trade by The Ingram Book Company

Table of Contents

Testimonials

Ray Gauvin shows unequivocally that you do not have to be on the front lines to experience the horrors of war and its effect on the human psyche. Trapped in a job no unwilling person should have to face, seeing day in and day out the casualties of war, the mangled bodies of our soldiers, the author is forced to see visions that can't easily be unseen later. His shocking assignment in Vietnam certainly set the stage for a PTSD environment for even the most hardened soldier, let alone someone new to combat. When exposed to such horrific images, such as he was, you can't ever unsee them. They are seared into your brain forever. You can only find help to deal with them. You see how PTSD affects not only the veteran, but also the family, friends and business associates. You don't need to be injured in war to feel its affects.

The author provides his own succinct summary of the book in this one sentence found within its contents: *When we American boys were growing up around the country, riding our bikes around our hometowns, going to a drive-in movie, and hoping to kiss a girl for the first time, how could we know that threads were being woven half-way around the globe in a bloody tapestry that would affect us the rest of our lives.*

It is obvious the author spent a great deal of time reflecting and analyzing his life's stories and how they have affected others. This must have been very hard for him, first to conduct the analysis, second to acknowledge his behavior, and third to write and present to others his personal challenges. It's difficult to image how the author managed to function in Vietnam. I shut down just thinking about the first body he had to x-ray. The author's description is so vivid … that I could sadly visualize them. In fact, I have a hard time trying to unsee them in my mind just from his vivid descriptions. I don't know how you managed to get through an entire year doing that job, let alone trying to unsee the bodies throughout the rest of your life.

I really liked the way the author linked Vietnam's history to his own. It really worked great. It's easy to see how the author's experiences in Vietnam affected his interpersonal interactions upon his return. It's unfortunate that Vietnam veterans never received the help they needed with issues such as PTSD until many years thereafter. Medical problems for Vietnam veterans tended to affect not only the veteran, but also the family. The author captured the experience of a Vietnam soldier's family well.

—*Col. (Ret) Judy Carroll*

The author's descriptions of his post-Vietnam PTSD life were so vivid and real that I was tearing up many times as I read through the book. His life has been so phenomenally stressful as he truly worked so hard at walking that fine line to stay sane and in control. This book is such a value to me and will be to any veteran that may have participated in the ravages of war as they were just "doing their duty" to serve their country.

—*Scott Smith, USMC Captain*

In a generation of men and women that answered the call to serve our country by serving in Vietnam "*A Soldier's Heart: The Three Wars of Vietnam*" captures the compelling story of one man's life, interrupted and radically changed by the war. It is an honest, heartwarming, haunting, gut-wrenching and redemptive saga that covers the tapestry of Ray Gauvin's life from childhood and rich heritage to coping with growing up and adjusting to life's complexities. In stark contrast to this is his military service, the horrors of war and the lifelong struggles in trying to live and understand what he experienced.

This is a great book! I loved the cover, artwork, maps and pictures throughout!

We got to see the deeper thread of the author's life, which was woven intricately throughout the book. A very fitting and heartwarming reflection on the impact our lives have on those around us. Love truly does overcome so many of the misadventures of life.

A beautiful preface. A simple but profound description of the evolution of man's desire to explain what happens as a result of the trauma of conflict by war. The history of your people was fascinating! Your life became more real because of the glimpses of how you grew up.

There were many important lessons from this book: The importance of family and being there for each other; the need to pursue avenues of growth and develop potential; the need to learn from mistakes and do better the next time.

—*Bill Honaker, Author, The Dead Were Mine (non-fiction about Vietnam)*

Of the millions of the United States service personnel very few have written biographical capsules of their pre-military life, wartime activity and post war experience. The relatively few exceptions are usually the work of officers, frequently field grade with well-known famous names. Enlisted ranks writers are poorly represented. This book is an exception to that circumstance and additionally discusses in some detail a military unit, Wound Data and Munitions Effectiveness Team (WDMET) completely unknown to the general public and also to most of the military.

This book is unique in many ways: it provides a personal biography of the author; it deals with the work of a clandestine military organization defining purpose and application; it deals with war zone post-traumatic stress disorder (PTSD.)

It is tempting to elaborate on the intriguing title of this book, *A Soldier's Heart*, but that would be an unforgivable injustice to the author. This book must be read to appreciate all facets of the intended purpose.

—*MAJ. C. Darrell Lane, MD, Major MC USA, FCAP*

Ray's "voice" throughout it is amazingly compelling and authentic. It serves not only as a history of experiences in Viet Nam, but also as a wonderful history of Aroostook County itself-- Chapman Street!!!! The first chapters are as fascinating-- and important-- as what follows-- and the photos are incredible.

The three "evolutionary" photos of Ray are amazing-- especially that quintessential smile in the second, followed by the third, which is a lifetime removed.

This is important work, not just for the remarkable (heartbreaking) experiences in country-- but the snapshot of an individual and families and the culture of the County...

—*Dr. Ray Rice, Ph. D, President, University of Maine at Presque Isle*

Ray Gauvin's new book *A Soldier's Heart* is a must read because it is an informative book for people of all ages. It will educate our young people and intrigue the old.

Ray's book in the beginning was a walk down memory lane for me as I grew up in Ray's neighborhood and we were friends. Interwoven into this narrative is Ray's very interesting American and Canadian background. As I read on, however, I quickly lost my heady feelings of memory lanes as I encountered the realities of the Vietnam War in this youth narrative and its impact on Ray's life and that of other young men of this terrible era.

Ray's story is not all doom and gloom because he didn't let it become that. His story is infused with his sense of humor which can generate a laugh for the reader even during these trying times as a young soldier.

I feel certain that his book will be read far and wide in Maine and probably in many other settings. Ray truly has a soldier's heart!

—*Ms. Susan Bailey, College Professor, Childhood Friend*

A Soldier's Heart is a firsthand account of the lifelong struggle to heal the less understood wounds of war. From a strong rural upbringing through the transition of boy to man we gain detailed insight into the preparation of Soldiers and the sacrifice that comes with service to country.

Ray Gauvin recounts a truly traumatic experience in Vietnam and the struggles of living with the resulting wounds. His resilience, loving family, and willingness to seek help most certainly saved his life.

This is an incredible book. Often the most vivid account comes immediately after the event. The author sacrificed no detail but incorporated the wisdom of the intervening years.

—*LTC (RET) Greg LaFrancois, Medical Service Corps, US Army;*
CEO Northern Lights AR Gould Hospital

A must read for those who lived through the Vietnam War and after. The life changing experiences of a growing boy to a soldier, husband, father and successful businessman are well documented in this heart felt and personal memoir of a soldier's soldier. As readers, we can only appreciate and sympathize with their struggles through life after their experience of war.

Ray was one of the lucky ones who relied on his instincts, and a very understanding and loving wife to get him through the nightmares that followed him through his life.

To quote Clausewitz in his military analysis entitled *On War,* "we are destined to relive the horrors of war if we don't take the time remember our history". What we do have is the history, what we are lacking is the commitment to do something about it for the hearts of our soldiers.

—*COL Don Tardie (RET), FA ARNG*

A Soldier's Heart is a fine story, and well-told. It serves an important role in shedding light on the men who worked in mortuaries and their own form of PTSD that many faced after coming home from Vietnam.

It is an honest story showing a veteran facing many life challenges after the war and ultimately defeating them and coming out at the other end as a generous, respected citizen known for an over-all life well lived.

—*Bill McCloud, VVA Magazine, Author, poet, and Vietnam War veteran*

Ray's book has filled a huge gap in my knowledge about the war and will for so many people as well as the inspiration to dig deeper when the going gets tough.

There have been many excellent books about the Vietnam War and its impact on those that served. The author has not only added to those works but he has filled a gap in the literature with a very vivid account of his Tour of Duty in Vietnam and its lasting effects on him which military veterans and their families will relate to.

… it's the author's account that pierces like a javelin with a unique picture of his incredibly difficult work for a medical unit (WDMET) that many scholars of the war haven't heard of.

Ray's assignment in Vietnam is hard to comprehend and the long-lasting emotional damage that it caused him is clear and pulls at the heartstrings, but his work there, whilst almost unbearable for him, has since helped save lives in both military and civilian environments.

It illustrates the bravery and resilience that is required by adolescents and adults alike to overcome the struggles with each challenge that life throws up, one after the other.

It also demonstrates that if you keep dusting yourself off and digging deeper again and again, you can achieve your goals. It is sure to be a great resource for Master's and PHD students in the future, but for those outside of academia it is a fascinating and inspiring read.

—*Brett Emblin, Vietnam Gear*

Gauvin's story will take you in from the beginning. Even more hyp-notizing than his experience in Vietnam is the coming-of-age story that frames the novel as a young man finding his way through many hardships, disappointments, but also moments of joy and triumph. I found myself at times smiling and at other times with tears in my eyes as my heart went out to him through all the experiences and moments of struggle.

Not only is this a stunning tale of a human life trying to make sense of all the craziness of the world, but it is more importantly a testament to the fact that we all have ghosts in our past, and it's OK to ask for help in dealing with them. In fact, it's essential to our well-being and the people we care about to do so. You won't put it down."

—Dr. Sarah Bushey, Professor, University of Florida

A veteran recollects his traumatic experiences serving in the Vietnam War and the emotional reverberations appearing long after in this memoir.

The author was sent to Saigon in 1968 and assigned to the Wound Data Munitions Effectiveness Team. This "exclusive team" studied the wounds of fallen American soldiers. In effect, it meant the performance of autopsies on the warriors, work so ghastly and demoralizing it was generally kept a secret. The experience exacted a terrible emotional toll on Gauvin, a suffering he recounts both candidly and poignantly.

"After a year in Vietnam, I feared I had lost the foundation of beliefs I had built my entire life upon. Was there really a God? And if there was, WHAT THE HELL WAS HE THINKING?"

The author would marry, start a family, and find financial success, but he was dogged by PTSD, a condition that expanded from mood swings to "all-out rages." In addition, he was diagnosed with dia-betes, a disease that may have been tied to his exposure to Agent Orange while in Vietnam.

Gauvin's struggle is lucidly conveyed—he paints a painfully vivid picture of both the horrors of war and the grim consequences.

And while the core of his book is a familiar one—there is no shortage of literature on either the Vietnam conflict or its aftermath—his discussion of his work for the WDMET distinguishes his contribution to the genre.

For those in search of a different perspective on the ghastliness of that complex war, this memoir is an instructive and affecting remembrance.

—*Kirkus Reviews*

Ray Gauvin provides a rich autobiography of his 75 years. The title is taken from the term used for Civil War veterans whose painful memories of war continued in their lives following the War. In modern times the term Post-traumatic Stress Disorder (PTSD) has recognized the burdens of military service that can shape the soldier's life long after active service has ended. Ray's book is a marvelous and courageous recounting of his personal experiences while at the same time addressing larger issues in society.

The work divides in three parts. The first is Ray's early years in Northern Maine. He provides rich memories of his Franco-American upbringing on both sides of the United States-Canadian border. Warm memories of his family and the Franco and Anglo cultures are mixed with recollections of the discriminations that were part of the society of the 1950s and of his family's poverty.

The strong influence of his father's mentorship embedded an entrepreneurial spirit in the author that shaped his life over three quarters of a century. His father's death at age 43 was a cruel maturing experience. Ray's high school years were filled with business experiences that provided income for the family and life lessons for Ray. He considered and eventually rejected a life of college preparation for a career as a Catholic Priest. Instead, he began college studies and saw his life shaped by the growing American participation in the Vietnam War.

Ray joined thousands of other young men in receiving a draft notice which place their prior life plans on hold. After exploring other options Ray enlisted in the Army with the expectation of service in a medical unit in either Germany or South Korea, if not in the United States. Those hopes or promises did not materialize and Ray was on his way to Vietnam at the height of the War. He was further surprised to find himself assigned to the WDMET based in Saigon.

And, what may you ask was WDMET (Wounded Data Munitions Effects Team? Ray quickly discovered the unique nature of the unit to which he had been "selected." The unit would evaluate combat fatalities before their bodies would be prepared for return to the United States. Often the dead soldier's body had been horribly mutilated. Ray's assignment was to x-ray the soldier's remains and assess the damage as part of a study to find better protective designs for helmets and body protection equipment.

The WDMET was not under the command of General William Westmoreland, the highly visible commander of the Military Assistance Command Vietnam. In fact, Westmoreland opposed the WDMET study as depressing morale both among the troops and among American citizens who were questioning the wisdom of the Vietnam War.

During his year at WDMET, Ray would handle 800 bodies as a member and eventually radiology unit chief. By the end of his tenure, Ray was near mental exhaustion. In his last weeks "in country" he narrowly escaped a bomb attack on the streets of Saigon. His superior officers gave him high marks as he finished his obligated military service and returned to northern Maine. He wanted to believe his gruesome memories of WDMET and Vietnam would stay in Vietnam.

Ray resumed his university studies with a concentration on business. He also met Sandy, a near neighbor in Presque Isle, and was soon a husband and a father. With Sandy's help, his business training and his entrepreneurial spirit saw him work in insurance, real estate, and financial planning, before moving to a career in payroll work as computers began to define the field. Financial success followed as well as leadership in the business, educational and charitable communities in Presque Isle and Aroostook County.

The Vietnam memories lived on, however. Sandy, his children, and his employees noticed Ray's unpredictable mood swings. For decades, Ray kept his Vietnam memories to himself. At last, with his marriage and professional career at risk, medical professionals connected his Vietnam service with his physical, mental, and emotional wounds. Healing took place and Ray and Sandy created the Aroostook Aspirations Initiative to counsel and finance County young people in their careers. Ray also reconnected with WDMET colleagues and learned how their work had in fact improved soldiers' protective wear and saved their lives.

Beyond studying the fascinating life of the Gauvins, *A Soldier's Heart* provides a vivid look at the Vietnam War and the experience of young men facing conscription-induced military service. It also studies the post-war consequences of wartime trauma and how one family survived PTSD and turned used its lessons to help provide a lifetime of service to its community and, especially, to benefit a newer generation of young men and women.

—Don Zillman, Emeritus Professor of Law
at the University of Maine Law School

Donald N. Zillman is Emeritus Professor of Law at the University of Maine Law School. Following his service in the Army Judge Advocate General's Corps he taught law at the Arizona State University and the University of Utah before becoming Dean of the University of Maine Law School. He subsequently served as Interim Provost and Academic Vice President at the University of Maine and President of the University of Maine at Presque Isle. He also served as Distinguished Visiting Professor at the United States Military Academy at West Point. He has written several dozen books and articles on military law including the two volume Living the World War (with Elizabeth Elsbach), a study of the American experience in World War I.

Aroostook County residents know Ray Gauvin of Presque Isle as a successful businessman and generous community leader. He often describes his gifts and service to the community as ways of "giving back," but few people know the depth of experience from which his gratitude grows, until now.

A Soldier's Heart: The Three Wars of Vietnam, is the story of success generated by determination to overcome unnamed obstacles, first as a teenager, then as a veteran. When [the author] enlisted in the U.S. Army for three years, he elected to train as an x-ray technician to obtain a valuable skill and perhaps avoid combat. When he arrived in Vietnam in 1968, he learned he had been assigned to a "hand-picked" exclusive team ... for the largest research study in wartime history. He was 22. [This book] is a memoir that gives voice to victims of not only Post-Traumatic Stress Disorder (PTSD), but also cultural discrimination and learning disabilities.

—*Kathryn Olmstead, Author, Editor*

A powerful and emotional read of an extraordinary life that simultaneously recalls both the resilience and fragility of the human spirit. Ray Gauvin's incredible journey, captured in the pages of *A Soldier's Heart*, is part history lesson and cultural awakening. But mostly, the story is of how one person who served family, country and community faced adversity, tragedy and trauma all the while persisting, using his keen entrepreneurial spirit to rise to the heights of professional success while never forgetting where he came from and the importance of paying it forward. This page-turner is just what we need at this time of challenge and uncertainly as a nation and world. It is a much-needed reminder of the precious life we are gifted and people surrounding us we are blessed with, as well as a reminder to be kind and understanding, as we cannot fully appreciate the experiences lived, and impact made, on those we encounter and embrace in our short time on this planet.

—*Jason Parent, MSB, CCAP*
Director/CEO, Aroostook County Action Program

[This book] is about the many people who served in Viet Nam and what they and their families faced when they returned. On many levels it was also personal to me. On another note, the book was very well written, it was real and didn't gloss over the realities of what you experienced and had to deal with after.

—*Donna Lisnik, Teacher, High School Principal*

Dedication

I t is with great pride and humility that I would like to dedicate this book to the following people:

To my children, who did not understand their dad's unpredictable, volatile behavior as they were growing up. I'm sure they felt they couldn't do anything right and that they were at fault for everything. There were times they probably were even afraid of me. A few years ago, I wrote a letter to each of my children, apologizing and asking for their forgiveness. I thank them for being so kind, generous, and forgiving in their acceptance of my apology. They are an integral part of my life and I'm so proud of the people they have become.

To my wife, who has earned the distinction of hero in her own right. She has followed me through my PTSD with its ups and downs, challenges, curves, hills and winding roads, along with all the heartaches and tears. She has carefully navigated the often-turbulent waters and taught our children that my behavior was in no way an indication of my not loving them. Her unsung devotion to a man that she could have left many times to escape certain madness has saved my life. I thank her for her unwavering love and support and her encouragement to tell my story. It was love at first sight when I met her those many years ago and that hasn't changed in the 50 years we have been married.

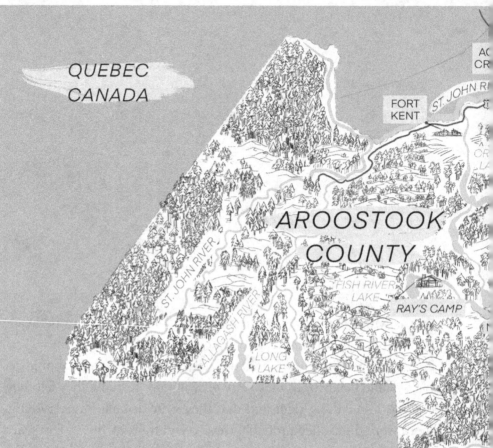

QUEBEC
CANADA

AROOSTOOK
COUNTY

FORT
KENT

ST. JOHN RI

ST. JOHN RIVER

ALLAGASH RIVER

FISH RIVER
LAKE

RAY'S CAMP

LONG
LAKE

MAINE
USA

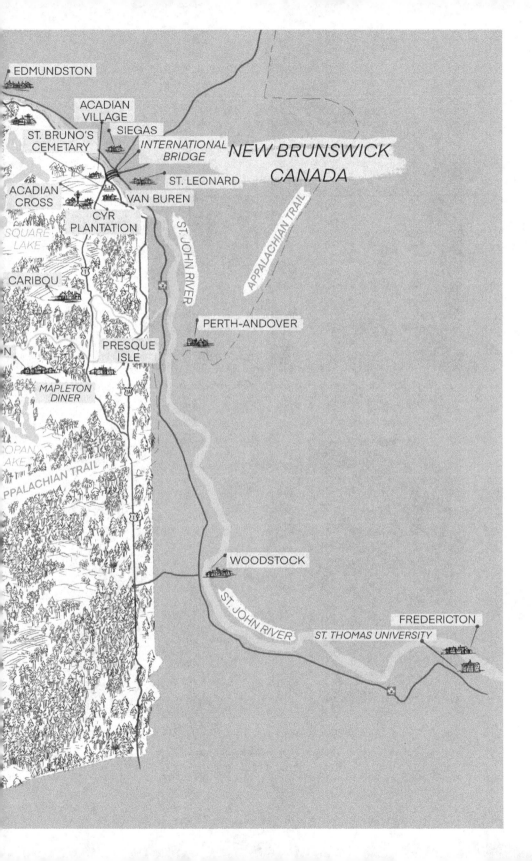

Top: Left: Ray Gauvin, proud graduate from X-ray school at Fort Sam Houston as a technician.

Top right: Newly arrived in Long Binh, Vietnam, 1968.

Bottom: About 3 months after becoming a member of the WDMET team, Tan Son Nhut mortuary, outside Saigon.

Preface

The military uses certain words to describe the aftermath of wars and what often befalls the soldiers who fight them. In the Civil War, soldiers coming home and suffering from depression were said to have *soldier's heart.*

In World War I, it was *shell shock.* In World War II and Korea, it was *combat fatigue.* It took Vietnam and its aftermath for the term and our understanding of the condition to slowly turn into what it still is, *post-traumatic stress disorder.*

Only "soldier's heart" still reminds us of the human being who fought for his or her country. From there on, the words become clinical and detached.

As with many of my fellow Vietnam veterans, I fought more than one war. There was my assignment in Saigon, and then there was the aftermath of Agent Orange and and the ensuing PTSD. Thus, the title of this book is *Soldier's Heart, the Three Wars of Vietnam.*

Every soldier of *any* war has his or her own story to tell. This is one.

Foreword

The Wound Data Munitions Effectiveness Team (WDMET) Vietnam was a small combined service research unit unfamiliar to both civilians and to all but a handful of military personnel who were informed on a "need-to-know" basis. The physicians and enlisted personnel were assigned to the pathology section subunit based on skills and pre-deployment training required to collect the data which would ensure the success of the mission's desired objective.

I got to know Raynold Gauvin as a radiology technologist whose primary duty was x-ray documentation of the wounds to be examined. We were very fortunate to have a cadre of talented, skilled and dedicated enlisted men who complimented the work of the three pathologists. Ray's x-rays were excellent quality making an invaluable contribution.

Of the millions of Americans who have served in the military from 17th century colonial wars to the present time there have been few accounts of personal life before, during and after wartime duty. Most frequently these biographies were written by senior-ranked officers.

Shortly after our unit began data collection in Saigon, I was assigned for one month to our WDMET Marine Corps Unit in Da Nang. Upon my return to Saigon, I was informed that I was now pathology section commanding officer. In this capacity it became quite apparent that Ray Gauvin performed his x-ray duties extremely well and was instrumental in the project's success.

C. Darrell Lane, MD
Major MC USA (Ret), FCAP

Prologue

In 1968, when I boarded an air-conditioned Boeing 707 headed for Vietnam, there were 536,100 American troops there ahead of me. Up until that time, the Pentagon and the American public had seen the war as winnable and soon to end. But the first Tet Offensive had riddled the country with fighting a few months earlier—it was a massive Viet Cong attack that broke the unspoken truce on the lunar new year holiday of Tet. And Tet II was already in progress. Tet changed the view of the war at home and news of the massive casualties brought the whole war into question. I knew I would be desperately needed and put to good use. I'd been trained at Fort Sam Houston as an X-ray technician and combat medic. And yet, the job description I'd been assigned only said WDMET. Other than those five letters of the alphabet, I had no other details.

The month of May in Vietnam means mostly hot weather. The rains start in June. For nearly two weeks in the sweltering heat, broken only by an occasional steamy rainfall in the afternoons, I cleaned latrines at Long Binh. It was a nasty job that smelled even worse than it looked. As I waited to be sent down to Saigon, we pulled steel drums up out of the ground beneath wooden toilets and set the waste on fire with diesel fuel.

Despite feeling heartbroken over losing my girlfriend, despite feeling lost in a foreign land, and despite the unrelenting heat and the smell of burning human waste, I couldn't help wondering, *What the hell is WDMET?*

On June 6th, I finally got my orders to report to Tan Son Nhut Air Base on the southeast outskirts of Saigon. We had just received word that Robert Kennedy had been shot while campaigning in Los Angeles and that he was still clinging to life. Knowing that our country was in such unrest back home was not good for morale. My plan was to concentrate on my job, do my part in helping my fellow soldiers, and then, in a year, I'd get the hell out of Vietnam, a country that didn't even want us there in the first place.

The next afternoon I was put aboard a helicopter and flown down to Tan Son Nhut, which took only a few minutes. It was a relief to leave the smelly latrines behind. A jeep was waiting for me at the helipad when I arrived, driven by the company clerk. I assumed he'd take me to headquarters where I would finally receive my job description.

"You Gauvin?" he garbled around a cigarette hanging precipitously from his mouth. I nodded.

"I'll drive you into Saigon," the clerk said. "To your billet."

"Saigon?" I asked. "Why not the barracks with the other guys?"

At least I could check combat medic off my list of concerns. Combat medics weren't put in billets, but sent to where the fighting was.

The clerk hunched his shoulders.

Side view of the trailers used for WDMET

"Tomorrow you'll meet Colonel Ostrom, our unit commander. He'll explain everything."

I started getting really paranoid. This wasn't typical of the military. If I were going to be assigned to a medical unit, surely it was time to inform me.

"You'll be given your own jeep for transportation," the clerk said. "And an M-16, which you'll be allowed to keep at the billet. I'll pick you up in the morning at 0-800 hours."

My own jeep *and* an M-16? For Christ's sake, I was an X-ray tech. After the first Tet Offensive, soldiers in Vietnam were allowed to carry M-16s. It was apparent to me by now that an M-16 wasn't a bad idea if I were going to live in Saigon. In addition to the Viet Cong sympathizers on every street corner, rockets were still exploding all over the city.

I assumed I'd be driven to headquarters the next morning and would receive my job description. But when the clerk picked me up, we drove to the perimeter of the base. There were three long trailers there, set up in a T-shape. They were old and a drab green color, the kind that are pulled behind Army trucks to carry freight.

"That's the mortuary," the clerk said. He pointed at a building next to one of the trailers. "There's another one at Da Nang, but much smaller. Da Nang takes care of the north. Down here at Tan Son Nhut, we get about seventy percent of the causalities."

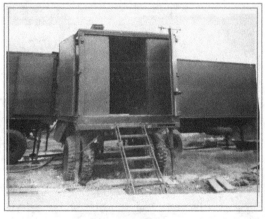

The trailers used for WDMET

Mortuary? We knew about the deaths, of course, but no one ever asked about how the bodies were taken care of in Vietnam. They just seemed to come home in the bellies of those big cargo planes. Not even the nightly newscasts or the protesters said the word *mortuary.*

"But I'm an X-ray tech," I said. "Why am I at the mortuary?" He tossed me a set of keys.

WDMET Jeep

A Chinook helicopter carrying the remains of soldiers to the mortuary.

"That's your jeep parked over there." He pointed at a jeep sitting in front of the second trailer. Its license plate said WDMET. "Think you can handle the traffic in Saigon? Just go with the flow."

"Why am I at the mortuary?" I asked again.

"Wait here for Colonel Ostrom," was his answer.

I stood alone as the clerk drove off. The mortuary was far enough away from the base that it had its own generators, which were noisy as hell. Why I had been brought there to meet my commanding officer was anybody's guess. As I waited, a Huey helicopter arrived in a blast of dust rising up from the nearby helipad. Two soldiers crawled out and then grabbed the straps of a large green bag. They lifted it out and quickly carried it into the mortuary building. It was my first glimpse of an HRP, a human remains pouch, or body bag. They came back for a second bag, and a third, and a fourth. A few minutes later, they climbed back aboard, and the chopper rose in the dust and flew off.

What the hell is going on? I thought.

A jeep pulled up in front of the trailers and a colonel got out. It was my commanding officer, Colonel Thomas Ostrom. I saluted him.

"I bet you've got a lot of questions for me, don't you, soldier?" he asked

"Yes, sir."

"Follow me," the colonel said.

WDMET insignia

Chapter 1

FAMILY & BOYHOOD

I f I could go back to a place in time, I think it would be a Sunday
at my grandparents' house in Siegas, Canada, in a room filled
with laughing uncles, aunts and cousins. This was my father's
family, and Siegas was a little woods-and-farmland community
just across the St. John River from Maine. My grandparents, Fred
Gauvin and Clara Desjardins, were part of a very large and closely-
knit clan who spoke mostly French. The Gauvins were typically
French-Canadian in that their belief in Catholicism was strong,
their support of family was undeniable, and a love of music was in
their blood. I felt a great sense of belonging in the Gauvin clan. The
surname can be traced back to thirteenth-century France, and yet
it's a more modern history that defines us. We of Acadian descent
still talk about the deportation, or what historians refer to as *Le
Grand Dérangement.*

The Acadians had come from France to Eastern Canada in the
early 1600s. They founded many small villages in Nova Scotia, built
dikes to reclaim fertile land from the sea, and put up grist mills.
For almost a hundred and fifty years, descendants of those first
settlers lived a peaceful and prosperous life. They fished from the
bay, planted hay, barley and oats, and cultivated apple orchards that
would yield barrels of cider. They grew flax for their spinning wheels,

since every home had one. And their large gardens were filled with vegetables. While working in the marshlands, both men and women wore *sabots,* or wooden shoes. They were a people who took pride in their homes, their farms and their churches. To relax, they loved a good fiddle tune and an evening of singing and dancing.

But life as the Acadians had known it would soon be torn apart by war. Acadia, or *Acadie* as it was known in French, became a political football between France and England in the struggle for dominance in North America. England eventually won.

British ships anchored off the shorelines of those villages. Given that the Acadians were Catholics who spoke only French, the English saw this as a dangerous factor. They demanded that the Acadians swear unconditional loyalty to the British Empire, or be deported to British colonies in North America and elsewhere in the world. Many Acadians had signed a *conditional* oath, vowing to remain neutral. But they would not agree to raise arms against their mother country if asked to do so.

The British didn't accept this, and thus began the Great Deportation in 1755. Thousands of Acadians—the number is estimated at between 14,000 and 18,000—were taken away in ships. Their lands were seized as British possessions, and their homes were burned. This expulsion was intended to destroy their very culture. The famous poem *Evangeline,* by Maine's poet Henry Wadsworth Longfellow, is set during the deportation. Evangeline Bellefontaine is about to wed Gabriel Lajeunesse when they are banished from their homes. She spends the rest of her life trying to reunite with Gabriel and, in the end, finds him dying in Philadelphia. Prior to Longfellow's poem, the history of Nova Scotia began with the British founding of it in 1749. After its publication and success, it was recognized that the Acadians had already been in Nova Scotia for 150 years. If it weren't for *Evangeline,* a fictional poem, what happened to the Acadians would long be forgotten.

Many Acadians stayed on in Canada, including my Gauvin ancestors, who eventually ended up in New Brunswick. But they faced hardships, which included hunger and illness. Some had lost family members in the deportation. But the worst fate lay in wait for the thousands of those deported on British ships, at least the ones who managed to stay alive. They endured the harshest of conditions and were scattered about the English colonies. Others were shipped to France, England, and even Martinique.

Many died, or were so ill they were tossed overboard.

About four thousand refugees found themselves in the bayous and swamps of Louisiana and were later referred to as *Cajun,* from the French pronunciation of the word *Acadian.* Remember that these were French-Canadians who had probably never even *heard* of an alligator, or ever dreamed the day would come when they'd see Spanish moss hanging from cypress trees. They must have been heartbroken, especially the first arrivals who could remember home so vividly, those green forests and blue rivers of eastern Canada. Even the ones who managed to remain in Nova Scotia lived with the knowledge that life as they had known it was over. A new life had to emerge from the ashes. In a way, that's a survival factor that I would come to rely on heavily in my own life. Some things can't be destroyed by war or even exile. Those Acadian family traits and traditions were obviously passed down through the generations to my own family.

After church each Sunday, we often piled into the family's old Studebaker and crossed the international bridge, from northern Maine to Canada, to visit my grandparents, aunts, uncles, and cousins. Siegas is only about three miles from the larger town of St. Leonard, but they lived a self-sufficient lifestyle in the country. They went to town only if they needed essentials such as sugar, coffee, tea, and flour. Everything else they raised in the gardens and fields. My uncles all owned farms so there were plenty of chickens, cattle, sheep, and pigs that made it to the family table. They hunted each autumn for venison and fished the rivers and brooks for salmon and trout.

My father, Hector, was one of the oldest of sixteen children. When he was born, the family was living in a cabin until they were able to build a simple house across the road from it. There was no indoor plumbing, so the bathroom was a three-hole outhouse. Pails of water for drinking and washing were carried from a well. When I was very young there was no electricity in the house yet, so I remember the yellow glow of kerosene lamps, with flat wicks and glass chimneys. Grandmother washed all the family's clothes in a galvanized tub, using a washboard. She did a lot of canning and cooking. Since woodstoves were used back then, she had the customary summer kitchen, a small addition where cooking could be done and yet heat would be kept out of the main house. Above the summer kitchen was where she kept her spinning wheel, that symbol of the first Acadian homesteads. But unlike the old ancestors who spun flax, my grandparents sheared their sheep. Then they carded and spun the wool.

Those Sunday tables were loaded with French foods such as *ployes*, the traditional buckwheat pancakes our Acadian ancestors have been making for over four hundred years. There were salads fresh from the garden. And it wasn't uncommon to see blood sausage and pigs' feet being served. The main courses on those Sunday visits were always generous, but it was dessert time that excited us grandkids the most. Even breakfast had a dessert time, not just dinner or supper. Grammie Gauvin would bring out several kinds of pies made from wild berries, along with an assortment of cakes and donuts. There was even wild hazelnut pie. Sometimes, she'd serve homemade ice cream that had been made in a hand-crank churn.

On Christmas Eve, there was *tourtière*, a meat pie, usually made with pork, onions, garlic, and nutmeg. When we cousins could eat no more and finally ran outside to play, we could hear the lively music floating out of the windows. If it was summer and the mosquitoes and blackflies were bothersome, we'd set twigs afire in a tin pail and then cover the flames with green grass to produce what we called "a smoke." Music, food, and laughter is how I will always remember my Gauvin relatives. They were a good- natured family who worked six long days each week, and then enjoyed their day of rest. I guess you could say it was in their blood.

My mother, Gladys Marie Gagnon, was born in Cyr Plantation, Maine, a small community just a few miles across the river border from my father's family. Even today there are barely over one hundred people living in Cyr Plantation. It sounds very southern, but you won't find Scarlett O'Hara on a *plantation* in Maine. Here it means something else altogether, that the settlement isn't a *township* or a *town*, but an entity in between. Since Maine was once part of Massachusetts, we inherited the word from colonial days. But in modern times, we're the only state still using it. There are over thirty *plantations* in the state of Maine. It still amazes me how war can infiltrate the most remote and pastoral communities. During the Civil War, for instance, when Cyr Plantation was booming with a few hundred citizens, they sent twenty-five boys off to fight. Eleven of them never came home.

Gladys outside her one-room school house in Cyr Plantation
(2nd row from front, 2nd from left).

My mother's parents, Fred Gagnon and Amedie Cote, lived on a farm that had been passed down to them by my great-grandfather Cote. The house was two stories and sided with aged shingles, with a large barn close by. As was typical of rural families in those years, they kept horses, pigs, cows, and chickens. The home sat on St. Mary Road, just off famous Route 1, which begins in the nearby town of Fort Kent, and ends in Key West, Florida. There were seven children in my mother's family, two girls and five boys. But one baby girl, Delcia, died at sixteen months. Mother grew up with five older brothers who liked to spoil her. She'd gather eggs from the chicken coop and help milk the cows, the typical chores a kid had when there were domestic animals. The shingled school she attended sat on a nearby hilltop, so she and her brothers easily walked there. In the winters, they went by sleds. She grew up loving horses. Her grandfather Gagnon had a farm nearby. When the snows came, he would hitch his horses to a sleigh and take the children for rides.

While Cote is an Acadian name, the Gagnon surname is primarily Quebecois.

Most Gagnons in North America today can trace their lineage back to three brothers who left France in 1635. Their names were Pierre, Marthurin and Jean, and they spent three months at sea due to strong headwinds. They opened a store in the old part of Quebec City known as *Vieux-Québec*. When the first hospital was built in 1637, *Hôtel-Dieu de Québec*, the Gagnon brothers helped build it.

Down through many generations, and over a couple of centuries, the Gagnon descendants eventually moved to villages along the St. Lawrence River, from Quebec City towards New Brunswick and northern Maine. The Acadian descendants of the Gauvins had settled by then in some of those same villages. As with my grandparents Fred Gagnon and Amedie Cote, folks met and married so that nowadays most French- descended people living in northern Maine and Canada are a mixture of both Acadian and Quebecois heritage. But we all go back to the mother country, France. It's said that all francophones in North America are related somehow, somewhere, if you trace their family names back far enough.

My mother wasn't as lucky as my father when it came to a happy childhood.

When she was nine, her father died of tuberculosis. There was no way Grammie Gagnon could keep a farm running. Her relatives would have had their own places to take care of. And her sons were still mostly teenagers. The family had no choice but to leave Cyr Plantation and move to nearby Van Buren. It's too late to ask her now, but maybe

Ray standing beside the iron cross that marks where the one-room schoolhouse his mother had attended had been located.

Grammie also wanted her children to have a different future. Once in town, she began doing jobs for well-to-do folks. Her three oldest sons found work in the potato houses to help support the family. As a child, my mother had to adjust to a busier world in Van Buren. She missed her father and the horses she loved. But this is the coin toss. Some kids grow up protected and happy, while others face daily obstacles. And this is the role fate plays in people's lives. My father and mother were now living in towns directly across the international border from each other.

The Gagnon family adjusted to their new "city" lives, and Mother eventually went to high school. Many people from Canada came across the border to shop in Van Buren in those days. Back then the weekend streets would be crowded. On one of those weekends, my mother's brother introduced her to his friend Hector. Mother said she knew immediately that this smart and handsome man was the one for her. I'm sure my dad felt the same way. Gladys Gagnon was seventeen when she married Hector Gauvin, in January of 1942. He was twenty-four.

Gladys and Hector's wedding day

Marrying back and forth among Canadians and Americans is still common today.

Young people attend dances and events on both sides of the border. Canadians and Americans form life-long friendships. But amazingly, even though my father was born and raised in Canada, he was considered American because of some old immigration law that was still on the books. Because his paternal grandfather was an American, all his descendants were also considered American. But I'm pretty sure citizenship didn't matter to the new couple. They moved in with my grandmother Gagnon, who by then had remarried as well, and that very same year, to a man named Frank Lebel.

Later that autumn, September 19, 1942, my father left for the Army. On his enlistment papers his occupation is *woodcutter*, which I assume meant *woodsman*, a typical profession in northern Maine and New Brunswick. I can only guess what my mother, as a new bride, must have felt to see her husband leave. Eventually, four of her brothers would also serve in World War II. It was a time when the whole world seemed to be fighting. The Germans had just surrounded Stalingrad, having no idea what lay ahead in the coming winter months. General Rommel, the Desert Fox, was in North Africa. And Americans were still reeling from the attack on Pearl Harbor nine months earlier.

It was this general unease that made a successful attempt by the Japanese to bomb the forests of Oregon, a week before my father left, all the more newsworthy. Amazingly, a small floatplane aboard a Japanese submarine was brought from its hangar after the submarine surfaced off the northwest coast. Its wings and tail were unfolded and it took off into the early dawn, headed for the foggy coast of Oregon with two fire bombs under its wings. The test run was successful in that the pilot saw his bombs detonate in the forest below. But no damage was done since the trees were too wet to catch fire.

Ten days *after* my father left, the same Japanese pilot made another test run, this time at night. While American newspapers were full of this successful and first-ever air attack by the Japanese on our country's mainland, those last two bombs were never even found. If it hadn't been for Pearl Harbor, it might have seemed like a Bob Hope comedy skit. But the country was still in shock, and the war was escalating. By this time, my mother learned she was pregnant with my older sister.

As it ended up, my father stayed stateside and didn't see combat. He also wasn't there for the birth of my sister the following February. But that's typical of wartime. He was instead attending Ordnance

Automotive School at Fort Crook, Nebraska, which is now called Offutt Air Force Base. He learned how to do maintenance and repair on military vehicles, including the Jeep, which the army had started using in 1940. But my father was not a well man. He had inherited through his mother's family, the Desjardins, a heart condition that would cut short his time in the military. He was at Camp Campbell, now Fort Campbell, on the border of Tennessee and Kentucky, when he was discharged in August of 1944.

Dad came home to find a job so he could support his family. My sister, Delcia, named for the baby sister my mother had lost, was by then six months old. Dad knew from what the doctors told him that *woodcutter*, the occupation he went in with, would need to change to a less physical job. Still, he went to work as an airplane mechanic at the newly established Presque Isle Army Airfield. It had been the local airport until the government turned it into a military airfield. The small city of Presque Isle, Maine, soon found itself a busy war center. Used as an embarkation site for sending aircraft to Europe, that base saw more planes take off from its runway than any other in America.

When the war ended in 1945, the airfield went back to being an airport.

My father tried selling vacuum cleaners and then Fuller Brush. He probably had no choice. He hadn't gone past the eighth grade and his English was limited, even though being in the army must have been one hell of a language immersion course. But selling wasn't for him, so he became a finish carpenter. I was born Raynold Aurel Gauvin on February 10, 1946, when my sister Delcia—or Del as she came to be known—was three years old. I was the first son. My mother gave birth to both of us at the Hotel Dieu Hospital in Van Buren.

The hospital itself had an interesting history. It was actually a Queen Anne style house that had been given to a local woman by her brother, back in 1938. She then donated it to a nearby Catholic order of Religious Hospitallers, with the provision that it be used as a hospital. The house had a wraparound porch, spindle work, single-paned windows, and a proud turret. There were fifteen beds, five Sisters, and two doctors when the doors first opened to the public. That's a pretty good ratio. No wonder my mother went back there for her next three children to be born. Of course, I can't remember being there. But I can imagine those long habits the Sisters wore swishing down a Victorian staircase.

Not long after I was born, my parents moved to Presque Isle, about 35 miles from Van Buren. They rented an upstairs apartment on State Street. The population then was almost 10,000 people, pretty much what it still is today. Presque Isle is one of the bigger towns in Aroostook County, up in northern Maine. It's actually been a city for several decades now. The name itself is French meaning *almost an island*. The Aroostook River curves around to meet the Presque Isle Stream, so the land where the city sits appears to be a peninsula

It was a town built on lumbering in the mid-1800s. In later years, given our rolling fields and hills, potatoes became a top industry. In the 1940s, Maine was the number one potato-producing state. It still ranks high in the nation for potatoes. When many people around the country think of this state, they think all Mainers grew up with an ocean in the back yard. But most of northern Maine is known for its rivers, lakes, and trees. Travel back then was limited compared to today. The ocean was hours away and many old-timers from this area never saw it before they died. It was not until later

The house at 67 Chapman Street. This had been moved from a different location farther up the street.

11

years that the younger generations traveled south to find jobs and discovered an ocean down there.

My father immediately began looking for a permanent home for his family. He was told about a house on Chapman Street that needed to be moved from its location to make room for three oil storage tanks. He bought a lot farther down the street and had the house moved. A family friend, Mr. Willette, was known for his experience in moving houses so he was hired to do it. There were few telephone lines back in those days, which made it somewhat easier. Dad dug the clay foundation for the house by hand, four feet deep. That wasn't what his doctors had in mind when they told him to find a non- physical civilian job. But soon the house was ready and he moved my mother and us two children into our first home. Our address was 67 Chapman. This was be the house that would shape my entire childhood, even though it sat on a street that many English- speaking locals referred to as "the French ghetto."

Always thinking of a way to supplement his income, Dad converted the house into a 3-family dwelling by adding two apartments. We lived in one of them. It had three small bedrooms, a small living room, and an even smaller kitchen. Over the years, two more sons were welcomed to the Gauvin family, and a second girl. We three boys slept in one bedroom and my sisters in the other. The tenants who rented the two apartments were mostly military people. In 1948, the Air Force had reactivated Presque Isle Air Force Base, so a lot of reassigned families who came to northern Maine needed a place to stay. And then, construction had begun just the year before on Loring Air Force Base in nearby Limestone. Since that year was also the beginning of the Cold War, this base was considered strategically valuable, given that Limestone was the closest point in the continental United States to Russia. Many local girls married GIs stationed at the two bases. Those young couples needed temporary homes. My father had a good instinct when it came to business. He understood that rentals would always be in demand with two military bases close by.

There were two major railways coming to Presque Isle, the Canadian Pacific and the Bangor & Aroostook. Numerous potato houses lined their tracks. The harvest was a busy time around those buildings as farmers unloaded barrels of potatoes off trucks and into boxcars. The cars had to be heated in the cold winter months to protect the potatoes. They were packed with blocks of ice in the summer. Potatoes from Maine were sold all over the East Coast. The station for the B & A Railroad was just a few hundred feet behind our house on Chapman Street, so we often heard the trains coming and going, the rattling of wheels along the tracks. In a surge of patriotism in the 1950s, during those early years of the Cold War, the company decided to paint 2,500 of their boxcars to honor the American flag. The top of each car was blue, the middle was white, and the bottom was red. Seeing just one boxcar pull in to the station painted like the flag was interesting enough. Several of them at a time was a downright display.

Northern Maine is still a pretty safe place to grow up, but back in the 1950s it seemed even more so. Kids biked around the neighborhood or played outside without our parents worrying about us. Not surprisingly, the majority of the families on Chapman Street had French last names. Most of their children had learned English by then, but the parents spoke only French, or broken English. You could tell by the names of the businesses along the street that the owners were of French descent. There was Frazier's, a small grocery store that had a meat counter, owned by Alice Frazier. Beaulieu's Hardware was owned by Ed Beaulieu. Robert Thibodeau owned Robert's Market, and Harry Michaud owned Harry's, which was a grocery and fresh meat store. There was even a dance hall on Chapman Street, a long building that was frequented mostly by GIs until it was closed in the late 1950s.

The neighborhood might have been called "the French ghetto," or "Frenchtown," by some folks, but it was a special street in many ways. We were all poor. But people took pride in their homes. There were about fifty houses along the street and they were all neatly painted. The yards were always well-kept, with flowers and shrubs. During the summers and autumns when the weather was good, families sat out on their front porches to relax. At Christmas time, the whole street was decorated with festive colors and the usual nativity scenes beloved by Catholics. No one had any money to spend on movies or restaurants, so neighbors visited back and forth to gossip and catch up on the local news. Sometimes our parents would gather on Saturday nights to play Charlemagne, a card game that was very popular among the French. The Catholic church and cemetery were on Chapman Street. Funerals were conducted at the church, and then the mourners walked to the cemetery for the burial. Everyone knew everyone, so in many ways the community that grew up on Chapman Street was like a large family.

A very young Ray Gauvin

Life in Frenchtown might have stayed very pleasant for me if school hadn't intervened. It was the worst thing to happen to me as a five-year-old. For one thing, I spoke only French and everything at school was in English. And for another thing, I wouldn't learn until many years later that I was dyslexic. This is probably why the other Chapman Street kids, including my sister Del, could speak English quite well. But I wasn't so lucky. When I started kindergarten, I was a shy, scared kid, an easy mark for school bullies. And because of the language barrier, I was called stupid by more than one of my classmates. Since the elementary school was a half-hour walk from Chapman Street, I always felt like I was from the wrong side of the tracks. Thankfully, my big sister was there to protect me. But that was not to last.

In those first days of kindergarten, scared and close to tears, I'd sneak out of my classroom and run down the hall to Del's room. Then I'd sit as close to her as I could. At least I did that until the principal paddled me for it. She was a very stern woman.

When she found out that I was walking home from school each day with my sister, my hand clinging to Del's, the principal decided it was necessary to break the bond between us. She ordered me to stay behind while my sister walked home first. Once Del was out of sight down the street, I was allowed to leave. I'd run as fast as I could to catch up. I knew then that I hated school.

All these factors combined to set me on a downward path. I was a poor student and took little interest in the three Rs. I guess you could say that I flunked kindergarten. At least, they kept me back and I had to repeat it the next year. As if all of this wasn't bad enough, I started wetting the bed. I was the oldest boy in the family, so it was a major embarrassment for me to sleep with a rubber pad under my sheet. I wouldn't break the habit until I was eleven years old.

In the autumn of 1942, the Treasury Department and the U.S. Office of Education had organized what they called the Schools at War program. It encouraged teachers and administrators of private and public schools to get their students involved in helping the war effort. Kids could do their part by buying war stamps and bonds, or saving money for their own personal security and independence. Grades twelve all the way down to kindergarten were involved. The booklet sent to teachers described a kid's savings account as being akin to "the casting of a ballot, and the performance of a duty." Student savings accounts would, it claimed, help maintain "a strong national economy," and even "preserve the American way of life."

The program was carried over into peacetime and, regardless of its patriotic rhetoric, it made a huge impact on me. I was still not six years old but I had my own school savings account. I realized then that I had to make some money if I was going to save any. So I started collecting pop bottles, the first of a long string of business ideas I would come up with during my childhood. Each week I'd bring my envelope back to my teacher with the bills and coins I'd earned. The school would then deposit it at the bank. That savings account, and my pop bottle business, probably rescued me. At least it gave me a bit of the self-confidence that I was desperately lacking.

Something else happened that first year of school that further damaged my self-esteem. The superintendent of schools paid a visit to my family. He told my father and mother in no uncertain terms that Presque Isle was an English- speaking community. He reminded them that it was a Maine state law, and had been since World War I, that English be the only language used in teaching courses in Maine's public schools. Some French-speaking communities, especially the rural ones, had ignored the law in the early years. But now schools were determined to enforce it.

French could be taken as a foreign language. Otherwise, no French would be spoken on school grounds. Therefore, Hector and Gladys Gauvin should be speaking only English at home to their children.

My parents had struggled to learn English, and my father was doing very well. But French was still their first language. It was all we spoke at home. It was the same situation in many houses up and down Chapman Street. Some parents did encourage their kids to speak only English, thinking it would help them succeed in an English world. But it was a blow to my father's pride. I could see it. He had taught himself a lot of English in the military. And he often read English books to better his understanding. He didn't need this well-educated man, a superintendent of schools no less, to come to the French Ghetto and deliver that message. But I suspect this is when my family began the slow process of changing the pronunciation of our surname from the French Go-VAH, to the English GAW-vin.

French-speaking kids all over northern Maine were having a hard time at school with that law in effect. This was especially true of towns along the river border, known as the St. John Valley, where French was more predominant. Some kids were made to write on the blackboard "I will not speak French in school," a hundred times if caught doing it. Rewards were given to students who tattled if they heard a classmate speak French. We were made to feel that we were somehow less intelligent than the English children because of the accent and language barrier.

But I must admit that I actually liked my kindergarten teacher, Miss Wallace. She was good to me, and she did her best to help me with the lessons. What I remember most about Miss Wallace is looking up at her nylon stockings and garters when I sat on the floor to pull on my boots. I guess that's the universal language for most boys, no matter what age. Miss Wallace and her pretty legs may have been my biggest incentive to know English. I soon learned to speak it fluently. By doing so, I lost the French language that my ancestors had spoken for countless generations.

When I was about eight years old, I started my own paper route for the *Bangor Daily News*. My territory covered all of Chapman Street as well as Bishop, Roberts, Main, and State. Bishop Street ran parallel just below Chapman, and a lot of Native Americans lived on that street. If anyone on Chapmen felt a need to look down on another street, such as was being done to us, then Bishop would be the one. Their houses tended to be run-down and shabby. They made us look rich. There were a few French- speaking families on Bishop, but most of them were either Micmac or Maliseet, from two local Indian tribes. Nonetheless, many of those folks were my customers and I respected them. They were good people and always paid me on time. We were all poor, as I saw it, even if Bishop was known for some rollicking parties.

It was pretty obvious to me by this time that all school did was get in the way of my enterprises. The paper route meant I had to get up at four-thirty every morning. I'd make a pot of oatmeal before I left the house since I'd be starving by the time I returned. Then I would deliver my papers and hurry back home by six-thirty, eat my breakfast, and get ready for school. During the potato harvest, most schools in Aroostook County would close so that students could pick for the local farmers. That meant I had to get up at three-thirty since my ride to the potato field came at six o'clock.

Ray's companion and best buddy, Ginger.

While spelling and math in school held little interest for me, I turned the paper route into the largest and most successful one in Presque Isle. I had been taught to be polite, but I learned to be persistent when it came to collecting money owed me. In those years, I had a dog named Ginger. He was a reddish color, part golden retriever and who knows what else. Ginger came along with me every morning. When you have a paper route, weather conditions don't matter to your clients. This was back when television had nightly news only, before all the modern technology that keeps the world connected around the clock. And that was if you even *owned* a television. My customers were eager to read the news each morning, and so expected their paper on time. Ginger and I often trudged through snow, rain, strong winds, it didn't matter. Once, we delivered papers in the midst of a raging blizzard.

My father continued his work as a carpenter, but it was around this same time that he had a heart attack. He would have another one a couple years later. It's possible he and my mother kept it hushed up so that we children wouldn't worry. They were like that, especially my father. But it meant changes in the family. Since he couldn't do carpentry any longer, and with our only income being money from the two rentals, my mother got a job as dishwasher at the Roma Café, a local restaurant. It was run by an Italian couple who had packed up their baby and moved to Presque Isle to escape Mussolini's dictatorship. Mom even learned to drive a car so that she could get to work. She later became a cook at the restaurant. The owners were very good to her, and to our family. We considered them friends. Since the restaurant was closed in the mornings, it was really a part-time job for Mom. She drove home after the noon rush was over and then back again for the dinner crowd.

Dad must have realized that he was playing with fate. With financial help from the VA, he signed up for a correspondence course from Beal Business College.

Accountants were not abundant in those days and it was the kind of desk job that seemed more suitable to his heart condition. He began his studies to become a public accountant, which is what CPAs were called back then. I've always had an enormous respect for what he did for his family, and ultimately for himself. Of course, we didn't know in those days that a desk job doesn't necessarily eliminate stress. Every accountant knows the pressure of tax season. In two years, he graduated from Beal Business College with an average grade of 96. That's not bad for a boy who was born in a cabin to a family of sixteen children, who didn't get past the eighth grade, and who taught himself English.

My mother was a great homemaker and a wonderful cook. But my father was the boss of the house. That was typical in those Eisenhower years. He was not a strict disciplinarian, but he ran a tight ship when it came to obedience. He had a barber's belt that

19

hung on the back of the cellar door even though it was never used. We kids knew it was there and that was knowledge enough. And yet, what I remember most was how much Dad cared for his family. He didn't have a lot of money to spend on us, but he had fun with his children. He was very musical and could play guitar and harmonica. He played steel guitar very well. We kids would sing songs with him such as "Beautiful Brown Eyes," "Frère Jacques," "Oh My Darling, Clementine," and "I've Been Working on the Railroad," which was quite appropriate given the frequent noise from the railway station.

When Dad was working as a carpenter, he'd come home some days and say to my mother, "Let's go on a picnic!" She would hurry and pack hamburgers and hotdogs. It didn't matter where we'd end up so long as it was a family outing. I remember one time we had our picnic in a gravel pit because all the good spots were already taken. But my mother must have realized all along how ill he was. After he became a public accountant and set up an office at home— it was between the little kitchen and their bedroom—we children were always cautioned to be quiet in the house and not disturb Dad.

We settled happily into the house at 67 Chapman Street. My pop bottle collecting business expanded to include old newspapers which I then sold to a moving company. They used the paper as packing material.

I joined Boy Scouts, which would also help me gain confidence in myself. As my newspaper delivery route grew, so did my ideas on how to make money. Some of my customers were doctors and lawyers who could afford to have their lawns mowed in the summer and their yards and steps shoveled in the winters. I accepted more jobs, even washing windows. Something else was happening that would affect me all my life. Those people took an interest in the shy kid with the French accent who was always looking for more work. They didn't just hire me, they encouraged me.

That was an enormous boost to my self-esteem. During those early years, I learned how to keep records, track income and expenses, and make a profit. With Dad's help, I'd decide what portion of that profit should be paid to me, how much I should invest back into my business, and how much should go into my savings account.

School was still on a back burner when it came to important things in my life. So I decided to start a vending business. New construction had been going on at the Woolworth's store, and also at the Zayre Department Store, both of them on Main Street. I figured the workmen might like a snack during the day, or a cold soda. And then, the Northern Maine Fair came to town each year by train. A lot of workers came with the fair to set up the rides and take care of the animals. For my business idea, I needed a good bicycle. My Uncle Elmer Gagnon had given me a hand-me-down green one. It was a good bike. I'd even taken it apart and Dad helped me repaint it. But it was old and cumbersome to pedal. So I used some of my savings to buy a new red one I'd seen at Sears. It was an investment back into my business. And then, what boy growing up in the 1950s didn't yearn for a new bicycle?

I fitted the bike with two baskets, one in front and one in back. There were no yard sales at that time so some folks visited the local dump to see what might have been discarded that could still be put to good use. Dad and I shared this penchant to salvage what was salvageable. On one trip, we had found an old Radio Flyer wagon that was pretty beaten up. I had been planning to buy one, another investment in my company. But I figured a new one wouldn't increase sales any more than a used one. We brought the Radio Flyer home from the dump and fixed it up. Since a rope wouldn't do a good job, Dad bolted a rod to the handle of the wagon, and then to the back of my bicycle's seat. That kept the wagon fixed in place behind me. I filled the baskets with items that wouldn't spoil. I had chocolate bars, potato chips, Drake's Devil Dogs, and even Whoopie Pies, that old New England classic. I then packed the wagon with Cokes, Pepsis, and a few Root Beers. I bought my stock at store cost and then marked up the price. I'd pedal to the construction sites, or

21

to the fairgrounds, and market my wares. If any of the men asked for hot coffee, I'd run over to nearby Beckwith's restaurant and buy it. Since that was a special trip, the price went up even more. None of the workers seemed to mind.

When I was twelve years old, Grammie Gauvin died of a heart attack. By this time, Grampie Gauvin had retired. They had moved from Siegas to a little house in nearby St. Leonard. It had indoor plumbing and electricity. We were happy for Grammie's good fortune since her life would now be easier. But people inherit more than cultural traditions, because the bad heart that had almost taken my father had now taken her. The family drove over to St. Leonard for her wake. Grammie was in a casket in the parlor, rosary beads in her hands. The shades were drawn and the room dimly lit. It was spooky to us kids, like walking into a haunted house on Halloween. The relatives had brought plenty of food for the mourners. My dad and uncles sat on the front porch to smoke cigarettes and talk quietly. I remember hearing my aunts crying.

Grammie Gauvin's death was the first one I would experience. I felt a deep sense of loss that I couldn't quite explain. On my next birthday, I would be a teenager. I had grown taller, but I was still teetering in that awkward space between childhood and adolescence. I preferred the safety of my younger years, but the death of my grandmother meant that nothing was permanent. Grammie had been the center around which our Gauvin family visits revolved. In my fondest memory, she's still sitting at her spinning wheel over the summer kitchen in Siegas, Canada, and I've just helped Grampie bring the cows up from the pasture and put them into the barn.

Chapter 2

THE LOSS

The same year that Grammie Gauvin died, our family moved to Academy Street.

Dad had bought a house that was being used at the time for meetings of the Church of Jesus Christ of Latter-day Saints. It was light brown and had a wrap-around porch. He paid $11,500 for it. This area of town was referred to as "the hill" and not just because of the elevation in feet. It was also an elevation in social status. At one time, it had been a field where dairy cattle grazed. By 1958, it was all residential. The best homes and the most successful people lived on Academy Street. Having spent my first years in the French Ghetto, on Chapman, I finally felt as if we were equals with the rest of town.

For days we loaded up the old Nash Rambler and moved boxes over to the new house. It was an

The house at 29 Academy Street. The wing on the right side of the house held two apartments.

exciting time for us kids. A moving truck came later for the heavier furniture. It was such a drastic change for the family that my mother was awake most of that first night, checking on us children to be sure we were all right.

The new house was L-shaped and very large compared to the one we'd just left. It even had a finished attic. Dad would later put two apartments in the back section, one upstairs with four small rooms, and one downstairs with three. But the main house where our family lived still had ten rooms, twice as many as at Chapman. The bedroom I shared with my brother Gilman was huge compared to our old room. Our youngest brother, Gary, slept on a twin bed in the hallway outside. My two sisters also shared a bedroom. The house had a gravel driveway and a large front lawn. As it was at Chapman Street, my brothers and I were responsible for mowing the lawn each summer. And we had to shovel the driveway each winter for the family and the tenants. Some people could afford to have their driveways plowed by farmers who drove into town with their tractors to do the job. But my parents considered that a luxury.

Dad set up an office for himself. It was in the sunroom, one of the nicest rooms in the house. He sanded and varnished the hardwood floor and put in a private entryway from the porch for his clients. The front of the room, which faced the kitchen, was all glass-paneled doors. Mom put lace curtains on them to give him privacy. It was a very nice office and he had certainly earned it. He hung his diploma from Beal Business College and his Certified Public Accountant certificate on the wall. I liked going down now and then to watch him work at his desk. He didn't mind as long as I was quiet and didn't disturb him.

As a matter of fact, that was still our mother's first rule: "Be quiet so you don't disturb your father." That wasn't easy for a family with three growing boys. But our father's illness seemed to float in the air over our heads, unspoken but always present. And so was the need for more money. But Dad had taken the necessary steps to better himself and his family. He worked long hours doing individual tax returns, and bookkeeping, and payrolls for small local businesses. We knew we had to be patient as his business and clientele grew.

When the Northern Maine Fair came to town in August, all of Aroostook County would be in a buzz. For me, it meant I had customers for my bike-wagon business.

The fair workers, animals, and equipment arrived by the Bangor & Aroostook Railroad, the one close to Chapman Street. The train came in around 6 pm and the local kids would gather to watch the activities. It would take the workers all night to unload the cars, most of them flatbeds. I'd fill the two baskets on my bike with the usual goodies, and load the wagon with soft drinks. Then I would pedal over to sell to the fair workers. My mother was always worried that I was hanging around "the fair people," as she called them. It's true that some of them seemed to be suspicious characters. But I never had any trouble. As I saw it, they were my clients, too, just like the doctors and lawyers up on "the hill."

I never did tell my mother this, but when we still lived on Chapman, I'd sometimes walk through the culvert on a hot summer's day to go for a swim. The public swimming pool was behind our house there, but on the other side of the tracks. Since it was a switch yard, there were always trains on the tracks switching cars around. The shortest distance to the pool meant walking through the culvert under the tracks. It was about six feet high and the brook near the tracks flowed through it. It was both an exciting and a scary route, but I often used it to get to the pool. That's when I'd notice trash scattered inside the culvert. There would be a dozen or so empty vanilla bottles and discarded Sterno cans lying about.

Sterno was used to warm the heaters that were put in the boxcars to protect potatoes during the colder months. Mr. Greaves, who lived across the street from us on Academy St., was a local businessman who bought Sterno in large supplies for that purpose. Often the people who worked in the potato houses would find a way to break into a storage shed and steal some cans. We didn't use the term "surrogate alcohol" back then, but we kids knew that desperate people drank it to get intoxicated, even though Sterno was poisonous.

Ray as a choir boy (6th from the left, back row).
It was the first boys' choir, established in the early 1960s.

I became an altar boy at St. Mary's Church in 1959, which pleased my parents, especially my mother. Father Royal Parent became another wonderful mentor for me and the other boys. He was also an assistant chaplain at the Presque Isle Air Force Base. In 1956, he had started a Catholic Youth Organization in Presque Isle, which happened to be the first in Maine. He even organized a hockey club for us and a boys' choir. A lot of things were coming together for me that would help with my low self-esteem. By the time I became an altar boy, I had been in Boy Scouts and choir for a couple years.

Scouting figured prominently in my young life. We boys were taught to be helpful, obedient, and kind. I began to feel pride in my life for the first time. I learned leadership skills and how to work well with others. School was still giving me difficulty, so I needed scouting.

Physically, I was an average boy of average height. But I was often self-conscious of my clothing. Unless I bought a few new things with my own money, my clothes tended to be hand-me-downs from any one of the multitude of first cousins I had on both sides of the family. I had started wearing glasses when I was quite young. My first pair was bought for me by the Lion's Club that had initiated an eyesight program to help those in need. This must have been difficult for my parents, proud as they were and both hard workers. But those were tough times for my struggling family. My parents would never accept welfare. But when it came to their children's needs, they would accept a helping hand.

Another bonus in my life was the week-long summer camp for underprivileged boys at Long Lake, in Sinclair, Maine. Called the Presque Isle Boys Community Camp, it had been founded by Joe Gagnon in 1929, when he was just eighteen years old. It was supported over the years by local business people and teachers, who also volunteered as counselors to help run it. It was a highpoint in my summer. My newspaper supervisor always took over my route so I could attend. We swam, played games, participated in sports, and ate popcorn while we watched movies every night. After lunch each day, we boys would be given a dollar. We'd pile onto the camp bus and ride to the local country store to spend the money on pop and candy.

I was a shy kid, so summer camp became a great place for me to make friends. And girls didn't attend camp, so that made it even more special. I had learned the hard way that girls might be trouble when it came to an all-boys idea. When the old Studebaker was cast aside for the Nash Rambler, my father had parked it in the back yard at Chapman Street. I immediately turned it into a clubhouse for my brothers and a few neighborhood boys. When Dad told me I had to accept girls into the clubhouse, I shut the operation down. I was still a couple years away from realizing how stupid that was.

All of the customers who hired me to mow lawns, wash windows, shovel snow, or weed their flower gardens lived on "the hill." They were the only ones who could afford those kinds of services. Dr. Boone lived a few houses down from us on Third Street.

Shortly after we moved to Academy, a janitor at school told me that Dr. Boone needed someone to mow his lawn. Like his father before him, Dr. Boone had graduated from McGill University with a medical degree. He was an old-fashioned kind of doctor who still did house calls. In the 1920s and 1930s, he would travel to farms and lumber camps. In the wintertime, he went by horse and sleigh. He then got a Model-T Ford pickup truck which he adapted for winter travel. He fitted it behind with cletracs, and then put on ski-like runners for front wheels.

When I telephoned Dr. Boone to inform him that I was interested in the job, he invited me to come talk to him in person. It would be my first official job interview. And since he was pretty famous around town, I was nervous. I sat in his study and our talk went something like this.

"I need my lawn taken care of," Dr. Boone said. "Mowing, weeding, that sort of thing. And in the winters, I'd like my walk and front steps shoveled."

"I can do that, Dr. Boone," I said. "I've already got jobs like that. I'm experienced."

He leaned back in his chair, amused.

"What are you planning to do with the money you make?" he asked.

"I'm going to save it."

"For what?"

"I want to go to college one day."

That was all I had to say. He hired me.

"Thank you, Dr. Boone," I said, and we shook hands.

Thinking back on that scene now, it must have been humorous for him to see me sitting there so intent on making the best impression.

After we moved to Academy Street, I started junior high. Country kids took buses to the school, but we town kids walked. The school was about three-fourths of a mile from my house. Because my parents were keeping a watchful eye, skipping school was out of the question. By this time, I could speak English fairly well, but my spelling was still terrible. This was years away from an understanding of dyslexia. For exams, I would memorize beforehand all the words that might turn up so that points wouldn't be deducted for spelling. I was always embarrassed to bring home my rank card. Still, my reading improved some. I was beginning to get Cs in a few subjects. I didn't care that a C meant average. That was good enough for me. I did like math class. And there was Mrs. Beaulieu, who taught music. She was an elderly lady who was very helpful and kind to her students, as was Richard Smith, the principal. He went out of his way to mentor me when he could.

A good teacher can affect a child's entire life. So can a bad one. Despite my minimal progress and improvement, I had some setbacks because I had some very tough teachers in junior high. I remember one of them, a male teacher, calling me out in front of the class one day. "Raynold," he said, "you are so stupid that you'll never make anything of yourself." As a boy still hoping to do well for my parents, and maybe even impress the girls in class now that I realized they existed, that was a major blow to my self-esteem.

It was at that time, amazingly, that I started losing my hair. I was still just in the 7th grade. Looking back, I'm sure it was from stress. Sister Mary Charles, one of the three nuns who taught catechism at the church, took pity on me. She mixed up a home remedy which was some kind of iodine tincture. I put it on my scalp every night for two years until whatever was causing the problem disappeared. The style for boys then was the crewcut, with our hair cropped closely to our heads. So, the biggest disadvantage of Sister Mary's tonic was that the red of the iodine showed through my hair if I didn't rub hard enough to conceal it. And I rarely could. It was not the easiest way to come of age.

If only there hadn't been such a thing as school, my growing up years would have gotten better as I gained more confidence. Thanks to my businesses, I was becoming a very independent boy, even if I was still shy. Fun was mostly free back then. In the winters, we'd skate on the Presque Isle Stream, which flowed into the Aroostook River. Even after the skating rink was built, the river was more exciting and daring. Sometimes, walking home after skating, we'd stop at Joe Gagnon's ice company and watch the men cut huge blocks of ice from the Presque Isle Stream. Many of those blocks were loaded onto the Bangor & Aroostook boxcars to keep them cool in the summer months when they were filled with potatoes. If we got bored, we'd bike across town to the Canadian Pacific station and watch the men turn the trains around. The CP men had to do it by hand. There was a large engine on a table which sat atop huge ball bearings, and that's what they had to turn. Even though they warned us not to touch anything, as soon as they weren't looking, we'd try doing it ourselves.

In the spring of eighth grade, I became very close friends with a girl at school. We didn't have any classes together, so it was luck that I met her at a school dance. She was pretty, with brown eyes and black hair down to her shoulders. Shy as I was, I still asked her to waltz. We started talking and things seemed to click between us. We could discuss important issues, like what we wanted to do with our lives when we got older. I needed a close friend like Marie. We spent as much time together as school and our family lives would allow. If she noticed the reddish color rubbed onto my scalp, she never mentioned it. And that's the sign of a good friend.

While school was still a hurdle, things were at least settling down for my family and me. Dad's accounting business was beginning to grow. His income, plus the rentals, was enough that Mom was now home full-time, as she wanted to be. It was a good thing, too, since a new baby was due that June.

When I think back to this period in my life, it's inevitable that most of my favorite memories are connected to my father. We shared a lot of hobbies that were even more exciting than raiding the local dump for discarded treasures. For one thing, we had model trains in common. I had two American Flyers that had been made in Connecticut. The first one I got for Christmas, and the second I bought with my savings. Dad and I would work for hours, side by side, on my model train table. We did that for eight special years. It wasn't just because I was his oldest son. He was an exceptional father in different ways to all his children.

When his youngest child, Lisa, was born that June, he liked to bounce her on his lap. "Look, Gladys!" he would shout. "The baby is dancing!" He taught my sister Del to dance by letting her stand on his shoes and follow his steps. In the third grade, when Del was struck by a car on her way to school, he walked with her for a long time after until he was certain she could take care of herself. When she almost drowned in the river, caught in an undertow, he was the one who jumped in and saved her. But he could be a tease, too. Del remembers how Dad would sing loudly in the mornings to wake her up when she was trying to sleep.

Once, for Del's senior prom party that she held at our house, he came into the room wearing her petticoats over his pajamas. It entertained her friends. My sister Diana remembers how he stayed up all night when our cat was having kittens. When the kittens were older, they climbed up onto his chair one day and raided his office desk. When he came in and saw them, he gently picked them up, one by one, and put them back on the floor. He often sat in the porch swing on Chapman Street and just talked to us kids about whatever was on our minds. His proudest time with his family was when we all went to church, his five kids marching down the aisle in front of him. We learned a lot from our father, and his influence shaped our lives forever.

If I had to pick my fondest memory of him, it would be a February day in 1961.

That's when I was the first in my Boy Scout troop to be awarded the *Ad Altare Dei* emblem. It means *to the altar of God* and symbolizes a boy's personal, moral, and spiritual growth. Before being eligible, a scout had to be of the Catholic faith, an active member of the scouts for six months, and have completed the sixth grade. I was in the eighth grade and knew how much this particular award would mean to my Catholic parents.

A photograph was taken of the awards ceremony that winter day. Four of us boys are standing proudly in the front row, our fathers just

Ray with his dad, Hector, at the Ad Altari Dei Award ceremony the February before Hector had his fatal heart attack.

behind us, flanked by Father Royal Parent, our mentor and favorite priest. Pinned to our uniforms is the Ad Altare Dei emblem, a bronze cross suspended under a bar and ribbon of the papal colors. My father is dressed in a dark suit, with a skinny necktie, the fashion of the day. He wears dark-framed glasses. It's easy to tell that I'm his son. Of all the people in that group, I'm the only one who is smiling proudly. I still regard that moment in time as one of the most memorable days of my life. It was also the last photo taken of me with my father.

August 27, 1961, seemed like any other Sunday. After church that morning we decided on a visit with our Gauvin relatives in Canada. With my grandmother now missing from the clan, there was even more reason to be sure we visited Grandpa Gauvin when we could. My sister Diana was excited about going. Dad told her to put on the blue dress that she looked so pretty in. He even tied the bow for her. When we arrived, my father's sisters put out plenty of food, just as Grammie had done over the years. This meant there was enough to feed an army. After we ate dessert, the men sat on the front porch to talk baseball. The Yankees, our favorite team, were playing the Cleveland Indians at Cleveland Stadium.

Roger Maris, who played for the Yankees, was one of my heroes. During that particular game, Marris hit his 49th homerun of the year. He was well on the road to beating Babe Ruth's single-season record of 60 homeruns. In center field for the Yankees was Mickey Mantle. He had just that January signed a $75,000 contract, making him the highest paid player in baseball. Yogi Berra was in left field, and Maris was playing right field. It didn't get any better than that. We had learned, thanks to a radio at my grandfather's house, that the Yankees won the game, six to zero. So it was an important day. The next day would be another one. After I delivered newspapers to my clients, I would get dressed for my first day as a high school freshman.

We crossed the international border at Van Buren, where my maternal grandparents lived. After a brief visit with them, we were on our way home to Presque Isle. The old Nash Rambler was packed since there were now eight of us, including the new baby, who was two months old. Dad usually drove, but he wasn't feeling well so our mother was behind the wheel. We usually sang songs during our car trips, such as "Ninety-nine Bottles of Beer on the Wall." But we were quiet on that ride home out of respect for our father. And then, the weather had cast a pall over the day, turning from autumn sunshine that morning to rain and fog by early evening.

As often happened when the car reached Dead Man's Curve, about ten miles from Van Buren, one of my brothers brought up the old story again. "Here's the spot where Ray fell out of the car!" Even as a kid, I liked to fiddle with things to find out how they worked. I had been inspecting the lock mechanism on the door handle when the door suddenly opened. I tumbled out of the car and onto the roadside.

My father himself had run out to retrieve me. The story lightened the mood, but still there was an unusual quiet in the car.

It was late by the time we finally got back to Academy Street. And the rain was now coming down in buckets.

"Ray, you need to go close the cellar window," my father told me. "I'll do it the morning," I said.

"Better do it now. Skunks might get in there tonight."

"Why is it always me?" I protested. "Why not Gilman or Gary?" It was a lament I'd voiced before, and it's one every oldest child in a family knows well.

Dad handed me a flashlight which I begrudgingly took. "Make sure the window is latched," he added.

It had been a long and exciting day: the Yankees winning, visiting my Gauvin cousins, Roger Marris hitting that homerun. But my mind was already on my paper route in the morning, and my first day of high school. I wasn't happy that I was losing my best friend, Marie, who would be attending school in St. Agatha, a town fifty miles away. We would now see each other only when she came home for visits. My younger brothers followed me as I went out into the rain to cover the window. The storm had intensified, with flashes of lightning and now thunderclaps in the distance. I hoped it would be over before dawn. Otherwise, Ginger and I would be delivering papers in a downpour.

The family said goodnight. The girls went into their room and closed the door. Gary climbed into his twin bed in the hall, and Gilman and I went to our own room. I fell asleep that night listening to rain beat against the windows of the house. It was after midnight when I heard voices in the hallway. I got out of bed and opened my bedroom door. Two men were carrying my father down the stairs on a stretcher. Someone must have called the ambulance, but I had heard nothing. Dad's eyes were closed and his face pale. My mother looked to be in a state of quiet panic. Del, at seventeen, was with her, offering support. I saw Dr. Helfrich, who lived a few houses away on Third Street. And there was my mother's friend, a woman who also lived nearby, holding baby Lisa in her arms. Mom looked over and saw me.

"Go back to bed, Raynold," she said in her French accent. "Dad is sick. We're taking him to the hospital. We'll be home when we can."

"I'm driving Mum," said Del. I nodded. It was a smart thing to do. It looked as if my mother's hands were shaking. I glanced again at Dad's face. He was known to his family and friends as a kind and caring man. He was a man proud of his family and of his accomplishments in life. I wished I hadn't acted like such a whiner when he had asked me to cover the cellar window. How long had the job taken me? Less than five minutes. I watched as the ambulance workers went on down the stairs, Dr. Helfrich following, and then my mother and sister. I heard the front door close. The neighbor lady took Lisa back to her crib and the house fell into a gloomy silence. I could have asked to go to the hospital with them. But I knew my father would have said, "You have your paper route, Raynold. You can't let your clients down." I went back to bed. I assured myself that he was sick, yes, but he'd be home soon. He was just forty-three years old. And he had been following doctor's orders by taking his nitro pills and drinking a glass of grape juice each day. And a brandy each night. The good news was that he was able to keep smoking cigarettes since it would help maintain his weight.

I did my best to fall back asleep as rain continued to beat against my bedroom window. It was just after dawn broke that my mother and Del returned. I was already in the kitchen making oatmeal and getting ready for my paper route before school. Del was crying and my mother looked as if it was the end of the world. I prayed that it meant Dad had to stay in the hospital for a period of time, that if it was bad news, it would be bad news we could adjust to.

"Go get the other kids, Ray," my mother said.

I went upstairs and shook Gary, who sat up and rubbed his eyes. Then I woke Gilman and Diana. Mom was in the living room when we came down the stairs. Del was sitting on the sofa, sobbing now.

"Your father had a heart attack," Mom told us. "He's gone. He passed away at the hospital."

It sounded as if her heart had gone with him. Gary, the youngest boy, burst into loud sobs. But I couldn't cry, not then. Dad wouldn't want me to. Funny how you can know the future course of your life in an instant, even if you're just a fifteen-year-old boy? I knew that I'd lost my best friend, my hero, my father. Now I needed a plan. When I got back to school, I'd have to start studying harder and graduate with good grades. No more fooling around as I had been. And I needed to find extra jobs to help my mother. She relied upon my father for all the big decisions. She didn't even know how to write a check. Dad was right. I was the oldest boy. I needed to be a man now. I needed to step up.

Chapter 3

LIFE WITHOUT MY FATHER

The Gauvin headstone, chosen by Gladys, after Hector's passing.
Both Gladys and Hector rest there now.

M y father had lived for five more hours after he was taken to the hospital. He was able to speak just enough to tell my mother and Del not to worry. His death certificate stated that he died of acute myocardial infarction, or a diminished blood supply to the heart. It also said that he had been suffering from atherosclerotic heart disease, a hardening and narrowing of the arteries, for eight years. It's a silent and slow killer that eventually stops the flow of blood to the heart. Maybe my mother and adult relatives who understood that Dad had already had two heart attacks, worried that something like this might happen. But to us children it was a total shock. There was nothing my family could do but plan his funeral. Many of our relatives had moved to Connecticut to work in city factories, a common thing for Mainers back then. The funeral had to be postponed until that Friday, four days away. That would give the relatives time to make arrangements before taking the long drive north.

We moved through that week as if through a bad dream. Relatives on both sides of the family and many friends filtered in and out, cooking, cleaning, and running errands. To make matters worse the rain never stopped. Of course, none of us went to school. I found myself wondering if Dad would enjoy knowing that on the first day as freshmen all boys had to wear dresses. I had been spared the embarrassment. My mother insisted we kids visit the funeral home for the two visitations a day, from 2 to 4 pm, and again from 7 to 9 pm. We were to shake hands with Dad's friends, clients, and family members. A rosary was said during the afternoon viewing, and again in the evening. Sometimes the priest led it, or a sister, or one of the mourners.

Dad owned just two suits and Mom had chosen the dark suit for his burial. It was the same one he wore that day we were photographed for the Ad Altare Dei award, a few months earlier. He had always liked dressing well, his shirts pressed and his shoes shined. His rosary beads had been placed in his hands. As I stood at the casket each of those four days, I was still determined to act like a man and not cry. I felt I had to set an example for the younger kids. But Gary, at nine years old, was inconsolable. We all were. We just showed our grief in different ways.

The weather seemed intent on making the situation even more miserable. When the day of the funeral arrived, the drizzle and fog were accompanied by occasional thunder. The service at St. Mary's Church was in Latin, as was the custom back then. I was a pall bearer along with five Gauvin uncles, my Dad's brothers. As we carried the flag-covered coffin into the church, it was all I could do to place one foot in front of the other. Mom walked down the aisle that day with the other children. That had been one of Hector Gauvin's proudest moments, his family walking that same aisle in front of him for Sunday service. But Mom was alone now, the bread-winner for six children, one still a baby. She even passed out at the church, as she had also done at the funeral parlor. I can't imagine what those days were like for her. She was still just 37 years old. And while we weren't aware of it then, her own health wasn't that good. She had high blood pressure and severe anxiety issues.

The church was packed that day, everyone wearing their respect-ful black. It had been the custom in Presque Isle that when Catholics died and the funeral service was at St. Mary's Church, the mourners walked behind the hearse to the nearby cemetery. But all the plots there had been bought by August of 1961. Dad was buried in the new cemetery for St. Mary's on North Main Street. Mom and we kids were in the car behind the hearse. We were followed by a long procession of cars, friends and family who had come to pay their last respects. Dad was given a military funeral with the typical seven-man honor guard who each fired three volleys from their rifles. I don't know the name of the bugler that day, but I wish I did. He was a soldier who was stationed at the local air base. As soon as he began playing taps, I broke down and wept for the first time.

After the burial service, relatives and friends gathered at our house for food, to talk, and to offer comfort. They had filled the kitchen with baked goods, casseroles, and pastries. I don't remember much about that day, but an older family friend recently told me that I was doing my best to serve everyone, to make sure they had coffee, tea, or whatever they needed. "You had already started trying to fill your father's shoes," she said.

The mourners finally left and we turned in for the night. After I said my rosary, I began going over in my mind all the things Dad had taught me. These were the lessons he hoped I would carry through my life. "Hard work pays off, Ray," I reminded myself. "Appreciate the importance of savings. Remember that integrity, honesty, and commitment are valuable traits. Have a passion for whatever you do. And do things for others when you can, without being asked."

A month after my father died, on the first day of October, Roger Marris became the first major league baseball player to hit more than sixty homeruns in a season, breaking Babe Ruth's record. But that no longer seemed important to me.

Our family did what it had to in order to survive. We tried to maintain as before.

When my birthday came the next February, Mom made me the usual lemon meringue pie. And then Del's birthday, even closer to Valentine's Day, meant the heart-shaped cake with the red food coloring. But the moments of sadness still found us. Mom's bedroom was next to mine. I was glad that the baby's crib was in there. At least she had Lisa and wasn't alone. But there were nights when I'd hear her softly crying.

My father's death had changed all our lives in an instant. Del had graduated from high school earlier that June, and had been set to attend the local teacher's college. With this new financial stress placed upon the family, she decided it would be better to get a job and help our mother. She went to work as a secretary for Maine Public Service. Diane, at fifteen, seemed to lose confidence. She began doing poorly in school. Gilman, the smart kid who had been so outgoing, slowly withdrew into his own world. And my mother, once content to finally be at home with her children, had gone back to work a week after my father died. The idea of welfare would have been the final blow to her self-esteem, and also to my father's memory. Faithful employee and friend that she had been in the past, the Roma Café was happy to welcome her back.

In the state of Maine, people often talk of "the county" up north as a place of hard workers and strong ethics. Back when I was growing up in Aroostook Country, it seemed even more so. In the days and weeks that followed my father's death, relatives on both sides of the family, the Gauvins and the Gagnons, stepped in to help out. So did family friends. They babysat, cooked, and even cleaned house and did laundry. When we kids got home from school, there was always an adult waiting there to make sure we had food and were cared for. They would end up doing this for years and never asked for a penny in return.

We were lucky to have these people in our lives, but we lost a lot of valuable time with our mother. She was busy with work at the restaurant, and also trying to figure out the logistics of being a property-owner in charge of five rentals. We still owned the house on Chapman Street, with its three apartments. Mr. Beck, a respected lawyer who lived around the corner, told my mother he would do all her legal work for free. He became another mentor to me, encouraging me to keep the idea of a college education in my future. It was too bad that Del, who was always so smart and quick to learn, had had to give up her own dream of college.

Even though my friend Marie was now attending school in St. Agatha, she sometimes came home on weekends. She was instrumental in helping me heal from losing my father. I was able to talk to Marie about my loss, and she seemed to understand how I felt. But, like Mom, I also kept busy. I remained faithful to my newspaper clients. Some mornings, Ginger and I would stop by The Roma Café as we delivered papers, and Mrs. Olore would cook me a big breakfast. That helped in that I didn't have to make my pot of oatmeal before school.

I did my best to succeed at school as well. I'd come into my freshman year as a D-average student, enrolled in a general course. I realized that studying would always be difficult for me. It wouldn't be until I was in my 60's that I would be diagnosed with dyslexia. I just knew that it was so damned hard to remember facts. So I bought myself a small desk to put in a corner of my bedroom. Since Gilman was often up watching television until midnight, I had privacy to study. I was soon carving important things onto the top of that desk. There were various words spelled correctly, math equations, and significant dates in history. It was as if by carving the letters and numbers into the wood, I was carving them into my brain. Repeating a word out loud a hundred times, and then writing it a hundred times, was my own method of helping me to remember it. Gilman was just the opposite, and that used to frustrate me, as much as I loved him. He could lie on the sofa all evening reading comic books, or watching TV, and then ace any test he had the next day.

My favorite courses were civics and math, and I loved shop. When I started getting As and Bs, a couple of my teachers suspected me of cheating. They would watch me closely as we were being tested. Once, I was even given a different test to see how well I performed without being able to copy off another student's work. When I got an A on that test, the teachers finally believed I was not cheating. At the end of my freshman year, Mrs. Stewart, my guidance counselor, took an interest in me. She suggested I switch from a general course to business, since she felt I could handle the extra workload. I liked Mrs. Stewart a great deal. As a matter of fact, she hired me as a maintenance person for her home. Her husband was a prominent attorney who ran a few times for political office. He even gave me a job tucking his campaign flyers under the windshield wipers of cars.

By the end of my sophomore year, Mrs. Stewart called me in again and suggested I change to a college course. It was a proud moment. Those hours of memorizing and late-night studying were finally paying off. I now had courses like trigonometry, geometry, science, and French as a foreign language, the very language my parents had been told to stop speaking at home. But I couldn't give up shop. Creating, tinkering, and building were good for my soul. It kept me close to my father's memory.

Dad's headstone had been ordered some months after his death from a company down in Augusta. It was put in place the following summer, along with his military marker. I finally went out to his grave one day when I felt I was ready. Reading his name carved into the stone seemed to be the written proof I was waiting for. I knew then he was never coming back. My mother must have known it, too. She evolved into a smart businesswoman. She learned early on that she was now competing in a male- dominated world. Often, men tried to take advantage of her when it came to fixing the shingles on the roof, or the engine of her car. She developed a backbone. She learned to ask the right questions and read the fine print. We were moving on.

A year after Dad's death, Del married and went off to start her own family. Mom decided that we needed more income to keep the household running. It was her first move toward independence. She turned her own bedroom into another apartment. The door was walled up so that we would still have privacy as a family, and an outside staircase was added so the tenant could come and go from a private entrance. We now had six rentals that were helping us survive financially. I felt proud that I was contributing as well by giving up a part of my earnings every other week.

I had saved $1200 when I started high school. By the time I graduated, I had $4,000 in my account. That might be why there are no extracurricular activities near my name in our high school yearbooks. "Activities" to me meant doing my various jobs, keeping busy with Boy Scouts, learning my Latin prayers so that I could take part in high mass each Sunday as an altar boy, and helping my mother with the apartments. I had made a few good friends by being in the Scouts and that helped improve my self-esteem. Some of my school friends and I started a short-wave radio club. I even learned to build the radios. This was a period in time when girls loved a "hope chest," a large cedar box where they stored items to use in their future married lives. Pot holders. Linen. Silverware. Dishes. I started a little side business making cedar chests to sell to high school girls. Dad had fixed up a small workshop at home and all his tools were still there. I used his shop to build the chests and the radios.

I don't know if romance might actually have happened between Marie and me if I'd had more free time. I just didn't think seriously about girls then. Like many good Catholic sons, I had been encouraged from a young age to become a priest. Many Catholic parents back then, especially the mothers, prayed that one of their sons would enter the priesthood. A daughter becoming a nun or sister was almost as good. My mother was no different. Nor were Marie's parents, who were very religious.

Sometimes Marie and I went for hamburgers when she was home for a visit, or to a ballgame. Or we took in an occasional movie such as *Mutiny on the Bounty* or *Music Man*. I could confide in her about the pain I felt in losing my father. To me, she was my best friend and nothing more. I had bought a class ring during my second year of high school, but it never occurred to me to give it to Marie, or to any girl. Romance would have meant a large investment in my thoughts and emotions. Even as a teenaged boy, I knew that I could maintain my heavy work schedule or I could fall in love with a girl. I couldn't do both. I had become that diligent in the wake of my father's death. Instead of asking Marie to go steady, I applied for another part-time job during my sophomore year.

The Zayre Department Store in Presque Isle where Ray worked while in high school

A new store had pranced into Presque Isle with "Fabulous Department Store" as its slogan. It caused quite a stir with the locals. This was the Zayre Department Store, affectionately known as Zayre's, part of a chain that operated in the Eastern half of the United State. I got the job there and started out at ten hours a week. I worked in

44

various departments, from managing the clothing and appliance departments to running the register as a cashier.

I even did janitorial work. But it was the ladies' lingerie section that offered me a world filled with both mystery and delight, and a touch of anxiety. The items in there certainly caught my attention. When I was at the register and women brought panties and bras and slinky nightgowns for me to ring up, I would blush red every time. It was when a man came through my checkout one day with a pile of silky panties that I was more stunned than embarrassed. As a matter of fact, *he* was the one who was uncomfortable, his eyes down-cast as he fumbled for bills in his wallet. I learned a lot about people and personalities while working at Zayre's.

The next year, I went up to 25 hours a week at the store. But during school holidays and summers I worked a full 40 hours. We were open around the clock in those busy days leading up to Christmas. It was in the small appliance department that I was at my best. Thanks to my dyslexia, I memorized all the literature about each machine, from Hamilton Beach food processors and GE electric carving knives, to Proctor Silex 2-slice toasters and Sunbeam's 5-speed handheld mixers. If a customer asked for product details, I could reel them off without looking at the instructions.

The store became so popular on both sides of the international border that when we went to visit relatives in Van Buren or St. Leonard, it wasn't uncommon to see a few yellow plastic bags with ZAYRE printed on them in red letters, flapping in the wind along roadsides. We employees were proud to say that we worked for the very first store in Presque Isle to have plastic bags. It would be over a decade until any of us even heard the word *recycling*.

I had a lot of respect for Louis Lamont, the assistant manager. He and I became friends. He was fresh out of high school with no plans to go to college. Yet he became a mentor to me, and encouraged me to get a good education. Our boss was Clint Waugh, a nice man with more than enough enthusiasm for his job. Zayre's was the kind of store that featured 15-minute specials. As a matter of fact, we all wore button pins that enlightened the customers. I remember one button that ignored what I was being taught in English class about capitalizing the first word of a sentence. It told the customer: *yes… you may CHARGE IT!!* The 15-minute specials were little extravaganzas. Lights would flash in a certain department and Mr. Waugh would get on the public address system to loudly announce the special. The idea was that shoppers would quickly flock over there to purchase the item before it was gone. After all, it was a "special." Mr. Waugh's voice was already high-pitched and shrill, so the special sounded more exciting than it probably should have. As soon as he delivered his message, he'd turn off the microphone and dash to the department that carried the item. Then he'd start marking the price tags. We were always amused to watch this. A few of us met each Friday after work at Aucoin's restaurant, and it was typical for someone to imitate Mr. Waugh announcing a 15-minute special.

Grammie Gagnon and her second husband, Frank Lebel, had moved to a house on St. Bruno's Street, in Van Buren, directly across from the catholic cemetery. It was always a hoot to visit Grammie. She had three cats she adored and a great mistrust of that graveyard across the street. She was always telling us how she heard ghosts making noises around the headstones at night. She'd point out an overturned stone as evidence, satisfied she was right about those meddlesome ghosts. *There* was the proof. It didn't matter that the stone had fallen so long ago that moss was already growing on it. It was during those visits to Van Buren that I met Shirley.

Marie was my best friend, and the rock I needed to get past my father's death, but I did not consider her a girlfriend. That's why I didn't feel any disloyalty when Shirley caught my attention. She had brown eyes and brown hair that she wore in a flip on her shoulders. Her mother's sister had married my maternal uncle, Gilbert Gagnon. They also lived in Van Buren not far from Grammie's house. For years when I visited my grandparents for family get-togethers, it wasn't uncommon for Shirley to turn up. Perhaps because we rarely saw each other since I lived in Presque Isle, spending time with Shirley felt like a respite from the steady responsibilities of my jobs and life at home. For whatever reason, I did not see it being in conflict with my friendship with Marie.

In late March of 1964, two months before Del welcomed her first child, Grammie died from an infection caused by her diabetes. She was only 58 years old. Like my mother, she had been born and raised in rural Cyr Plantation. And like my mother, she had lost her husband young, at the age of 28, and was left to raise a large family on her own. We drove over to Van Buren for each night of the wake, and again for the funeral. It must have been difficult for my mother to have lost her brother, husband, and mother in such a short space of time. Amedie Cote Gagnon Lebel's funeral service was at the Church of St. Bruno-St. Remi. The burial was in St. Bruno's Cemetery, the one just across the street from the house where my step-grandfather Lebel would now live alone.

As we drove back to Presque Isle that night, I remembered how my mother would put me on the train to Van Buren when I was no more than five years old. I would spend a few hours visiting Grammie Lebel. Then Grammie would put me back on the train and I'd ride home again. The conductor, or some guardian angel who wasn't busy, must have watched out for me. But that was the umbrella of safety we lived under back then. When I grew older, I would sometimes pedal my bike along Route 1, a narrow road bordered by potato fields, barns, and curious cows. I would pass through Cyr Plantation on my way to visit Grammie. Now she was gone. When I said my rosary the night of the funeral, I added her name to the list of people I should pray for. But I had to smile since it would be Grammie Lebel's first night in St. Bruno's Cemetery. At that very minute, she was probably scolding the other ghosts for knocking over headstones.

The summer before I began my senior year. I had been seeing more of Shirley on visits to my relatives in Van Buren. I even kissed her, the first time I'd ever kissed a girl. It was like one of those flashing-light specials at Zayre's. My world suddenly lit up.

Coincidence plays a role in most lives and mine was no different. That autumn of 1964, two young Catholic girls from northern Maine visited Mercy Hospital's nursing program down in Portland. They were both looking for a good nursing school to attend once they graduated from high school. They ended up on the same bus headed back north. As fate would have it, they even shared a seat. As often happens when young girls meet, the talk got around to the special boys in their lives. It seems in this case there was only one boy. *Me.* Marie was not happy that her fellow bus passenger, Shirley, had mentioned seeing quite a bit of a boy from Presque Isle named Raynold Gauvin. Did she happen to know him? Marie not only knew me, but in *her* mind, I was her boyfriend.

Where was St. Christopher, the patron saint of travelers, when you needed him? That was the end of my friendship with Marie. A couple of months later, she began dating a nice boy who had been giving her the eye for some time. She didn't know it then, but he was her future husband.

Shirley and I dated through our senior year, but I never gave her my ring. There was something about committing so young that held me back. I still had college ahead. I was already doubtful that the priesthood was for me. But my mother kept pushing me in that direction. I had gotten good grades my senior year but didn't score well on my college boards. I figured that would really mess things up for me. My guidance counselor felt sure I'd be accepted anyway. I considered getting an accounting degree from Husson College, in Bangor. This would distance me even more from the priesthood. In May of 1965, I drove down to Bangor for an interview at Husson College. I was later accepted.

That might have been the end of it, but Father Albert, a priest at my parish, encouraged me to apply to St. Thomas University, in Fredericton. After two years in a liberal arts program there, I could then decide if I wanted to enter the priesthood. I applied. And even though I had enough money saved to pay for my first year of college, regardless of where I went, I also applied for scholarships my senior year. The Kiwanis Club had one, and so did the Daughters of Isabella and the Knights of Columbus. A very prestigious one was the Mark and Emily Turner Scholarship for $1,000. I figured a kid from a well-connected family would get that one but applied anyway. As it turned out, I got them all.

In June, I took Shirley to my senior prom. Embarrassingly, my mother insisted on driving me to Van Buren to pick her up. It hurt that she didn't trust me. After all, I had turned 18 that year. Hell, I'd even registered for the draft right after my birthday, as was required of all young men at that time.

The sad truth was that my mother and I had started locking horns not long after Dad died. It felt as if I'd gone from being her son to being a financial partner and handyman for the rentals. Oldest sons are often called upon to be more responsible than the younger kids. I understood that the car was her only means to drive to work. I also felt I had earned some freedom and maybe even respect. I didn't think I was getting either. And Dad wasn't there to act as a buffer between my mother and me. Had he been, our problems likely wouldn't have arisen in the first place.

Once we got back to Presque Isle she did let me drive to the prom without her along as chauffeur. But I was feeling suffocated by then and anxious to break away from those French apron strings. I knew my mother had had tough circumstances in her life without my father, but there was only so much guilt over her situation that I could shoulder. I wanted to live my own life.

Ray and Gladys on the day of Ray's high school graduation

When an acceptance letter came from St. Thomas University, I was ready to get out of Dodge. My high school graduation was a proud moment for me. I had begun as a D-student and yet would soon be on my way to college. When I was presented with the scholarships I'd won, it was the Mark & Emily Turner that filled me with the most pride. Marie even congratulated me, and later introduced Shirley and me to her steady boyfriend. My mother must have been pleased when WAGM, the local news station, came out to interview her son that night. But I wished my father had been there. He'd been right. Hard work pays off.

It was time now to tie up loose ends and get ready for what lay ahead. The country as a whole was looking to the future, to the day when it would send the first man to the moon and hopefully before the Russians. In March of that year, a Russian cosmonaut had become the first man to walk in space. In June, astronaut Edward White floated for twenty-two minutes in the blackness surrounding Gemini 4. The world I had grown up in, those Eisenhower years of the 1950s, was dissolving with each new invention, each mile-stone, each breakthrough in medicine and technology. Trouble was brewing on the horizon as well. The first American combat troops had been sent to Vietnam, a little country somewhere in Southeast Asia that was popping up more and more in the nightly news.

I felt ready for the future. I had built a solid foundation beneath me. My time with the Boy Scouts had ended when I turned eigh-teen, the year before. I had spent many good, character-building years with that troop. I left with every merit badge they offered except swimming. I even kept up my paper route the summer after I graduated. I had delivered the news to my customers for a decade and they, in turn, had helped finance my first year of college. Now it was time for brother Gilman to take over my route. I had already given my bicycle to my younger brothers. It was a symbol of my childhood that was now over. I suspect the Red Flyer wagon went back to the dump, this time for good.

I took money from my savings to buy myself some clothes and a suitcase to pack them in. Since Father Albert had been instrumental in pushing me toward St. Thomas University and eventual priest-hood, he drove me to the campus in late August. On the way, he reminded me that if I did well academically for my first two years, the Roman Catholic Diocese of Portland would pay for the rest of my education. I didn't tell him what Shirley already knew, that I had serious doubts the priesthood was for me. And I certainly hadn't told my mother, who was still pinning her hopes of having given birth to a priest onto her oldest son. I could have gone to Husson and aimed for more straight forward future in accounting. But crossing the international border and going to Fredericton, New Brunswick, seemed to offer more distance and freedom, even though it was actually closer than Bangor. It was as if that border was an invisible line drawn in the sand. On one side of the line was my past, with good and bad memories combined. On the other side was my still unwritten future.

Chapter 4

COLLEGE & THE DRAFT

Fredericton was twice the size of Presque Isle with a population of about 20,000. The St. John River that separated my paternal and maternal grandparents by nationality back upstream at Van Buren and St. Leonard, now ran directly through the town. I was painfully aware of my Acadian connection with Fredericton, and in some ways felt I was reclaiming my right to be there. Some of my Acadian ancestors who had been driven from their homes by the British in 1755, had relocated to small settlements along the St. John River. They had even taken the oath of alliance that England demanded, and thus were on Great Britain's side in the American Revolution. But as soon as the war was over, English-speaking Loyalists who had fled the American Revolution in 1783 and headed north to Canada were given the Acadian land at Ste. Anne's Point, where Fredericton sits today. The French-speaking Acadians were again forced to move on. It is a terrible irony that although the Loyalists were given land grants that appropriated Acadian land, many of them had left behind all their worldly goods. and spent the first winter in tents and crude temporary shelters. Those who were less well-to-do died that first harsh Canadian winter. The Loyalist Cemetery that lies on the south side of the St. John is lasting testimony to their hardships and mortalities.

St. Thomas University's motto was *Doce Bonitatem Scientiam et Disciplinam*. Teach Me Goodness, Knowledge and Discipline. The setting was bucolic, on a steep hill overlooking the river. The school actually sat a short distance away from the University of New Brunswick's "den of atheists," about a half mile up the road. In 1965, it had 22 faculty members, 4 buildings, and less than 500 students. And yet, within no time of my arrival, it was as if everything I'd learned from my father went down the drain, my study habits, and even my eating habits. I had broken the apron strings all right, but I also broke a lot of promises I'd made to myself about my future.

I hope I came away after a year with at least a little *Goodness*.

My roommate in Harrington Hall was a kid from St. John, New Brunswick and a great guy. We bonded immediately. He had been raised on a farm in New Brunswick and, like me, his life had been limited. Together we decided to explore all the promises that our newfound freedom offered. In no time, we had mastered the art of climbing out our dorm window and frequenting the nearby pubs. Fredericton was a conservative town and very Anglo in its sensibility and customs. Fish & chips was on most menus in the local restaurants and it soon became my favorite food. Conservative or not, there were a number of taverns that stayed busy when night fell. It was not unusual to see priests from the St. Thomas faculty in those same bars, without their priest collars. At first this was very disconcerting for me. I had been raised to think priests were pious and closer to God than us mortals. Mike and I kept our distance for fear they might recognize us as students, although I doubted they would dare turn us in. I was tempted to let my mother know about it, though there were plenty of devout priests like Father Parent and Father Albert to keep her happy.

The hardworking high school student I'd become seemed to disappear overnight. I had been operating under such pressure for so many years that the dam simply broke. I was also subconsciously

54

rebelling against the priesthood. If I did well for two years at STU, after all, those seminary doors would open to me. I began skipping classes. I wasn't doing any homework or studying anyway, so how could I possibly go to class? The Dean of Men was an Irish-born gentleman named Mr. Rigby. He was perpetually walking the halls in our dorm, keeping an eye on things. Since it was too risky for me to return to my room, I'd head down to the library at the University of New Brunswick. I liked that place. It was filled with magazines and newspapers I had never seen before. They were probably magazines that my mother would not have approved of me reading. But I read them anyway. I was a free man now.

I didn't try out for any sports, but I was getting exercise climbing in and out of that dorm window in order to frequent the bars, or take in a campus hockey game. And then, when we needed milk with our banana sandwiches— Mr. Rigby had introduced us to this delicacy—we raided the machines in the dining hall. Mr. Rigby seemed eager to talk some sense into me, and when I didn't take his advice to attend classes, he turned to

The Thomists record album. The Thomists was the band Mr. Rigby formed at St. Thomas University and encouraged Ray to try out for.

music. After becoming Dean of Men, he had formed a band called "The Thomists," named in deference to our university and St. Thomas Aquinas. Hoping to motivate me, Mr. Rigby encouraged me to take trombone lessons and try out for the band once I was good enough. I rented a trombone and he gave me just two lessons before he suggested I take it back to the music store. "I'm sorry, Raynold, but you're tone deaf," he said. So I returned to my previous extracurricular activities of frequenting the pubs and eating fish & chips. The Thomists were better off without me.

I wasn't a long distance from home in mileage, but I was in spirit. I thought of the house on Academy Street and my two brothers in my old bedroom. I thought of Lisa, the baby who would never know her father. She was then four years old and had a habit of clinging to me when I picked her up. She would clutch my hair with her little hands and plant kisses all over my face. I assumed it was a father's comfort that she was instinctively reaching out for. I had told Gilman and Gary to pay attention to her while I was gone. Del had her own baby now, a toddler. Diane was in her senior year of high school. She'd be there, too, for Lisa.

Missing home and siblings as I was, I began to write letters every day to Shirley. This was an arduous task because of my dyslexia. I should have gotten credit for those letters I wrote, a kind of independent study. Given the quality of my handwriting, it probably took Shirley as long to read them as it took me to write them. I always looked forward to her letters back to me, and that's when I knew that I was very serious about her. I figured I might even be in love. Every other weekend I hitch- hiked the 150 miles up to Van Buren to visit her. The driver who picked me up would drop me off at the international bridge at St. Leonard. I'd walk past Canadian customs, cross over the river, and then go through customs on the American side. The more rides I bummed to see Shirley, the more doubtful I was about the priesthood.

For sleeping arrangements while I was in Van Buren, I'd get a room at the Hammond Hotel, an expensive investment for a college student's budget. Those years of careful accounting and saving that I'd learned from my father also seemed to have evaporated. But there was logic to my spending. Next door to the Hammond was the Gaiety Theater, and the Modern Theater was just across the street. Since Shirley and I liked movies, this meant convenience along with our entertainment. Besides, I had months to worry about how to pay for college the following year. Sometimes, out of guilt, I'd stop in to see my step-grandfather Lebel and say hello. I had never been close to him but I knew Grammie would approve of my showing him that respect. Before heading back to campus, I'd take time to visit her headstone in the cemetery across the street. The only downside of my trips up to Van Buren to see Shirley was that, while I was falling in love with *her*, she still wasn't ready to fully commit to *me*.

When I took my final exams, I remember an encounter outside a classroom door with one of my professors. I was there to take my final in Biblical History. "You missed most of the classes, Mr. Gauvin," he said. "Why are you bothering to take the final?" It was a damn good question. I smiled and said, "I guess I'm hoping for a lot of luck." Now it was his turn to smile. "Well then, good luck," he said. I flunked the class, of course. As a matter of fact, I flunked them all but two. I passed Ancient History by the proverbial hair. And I also not only passed Logic. I did very well in it

In spite of that spectacular failure, my first year of college was not a total waste. I learned that I was tone deaf and should never rent another trombone, or *any* musical instrument. I learned to love hockey, fish & chips, and banana sandwiches. I learned to appreciate classical music and jazz, despite my apparent insensitivity to musical pitch. I learned that priests are human, and I learned that if you don't work hard and apply yourself, as I had done in high school, the results would be less than stellar. And I pretty much knew for certain that I didn't want to become a priest. At the end of the school year, when I packed up my things and headed for home, I had less than a thousand dollars left in my savings account.

My arrival home had not been met with fanfare. My mother felt that I should begin contributing to the family income again. I didn't see how I could save for my second year of college and also help her. She still had the six rentals and her own income from Roma Café. Diana was nineteen years old by that time and had been babysitting. Gilman was eighteen and mowing a few lawns. He and Gary, then fourteen, still had my old paper route. But my younger siblings had not been as keen to become young entrepreneurs as I had. I might have been the oldest son, but my mother's concept of what that meant was now different from my own. I felt I'd done my share in years past. Tone deaf or not, I was hearing a different drummer.

My mother disagreed wholeheartedly. In various conversations we had about finances and the priesthood, there was more than one pot or pan tossed at me as I fled up the stairs or out the front door. I knew then I had to move out, even if that meant the expense of a place to stay. I had often felt over the years that even though my mother loved me, there was a current of resentment on her part that sometimes flowed between us. One winter's day when I was a sophomore in high school, I had shoveled the yard after a heavy snowfall. When I finished and came inside, I was exhausted. It was a big yard and the snow had been deep. Instead of thanking me, my mother said, "Ray, you did that work just to show off in front of the neighbors." That hurt for a long time afterwards. But it didn't stop me from shoveling the yard the next time it snowed. I wasn't ready to adjust back into the old patterns so quickly. I was twenty years old. I wanted to be in control of my life for a change. I found a job at the Aroostook State Farm, one of the experimental farms that were part of the University of Maine's ongoing projects created to study problems affecting Maine's potato industry. I became an assistant to Robert Newman, from Cornell University, in his research on ladybugs and their effects on aphids. The job was forty hours a week from Monday to Friday. It paid a little better than the minimum wage, which was $1.25 an hour. . .

With a job secured, I went around town looking for a place to stay. By this time, it had become unbearable for me at home. Even my brothers and sisters seemed to be taking my mother's side, all except little Lisa, who was too young to understand. I found a room on Pleasant Street at a place called Martin's Manor, a lot fancier sounding than it actually was.

There was a twin bed in the room, an easy chair, a small kitchen table, and a cabinet with dishes and utensils. Two hot plates were included in the rent so that I could cook meals in the room. Bedding and towels were also provided. I assumed this generosity of provisions was because many of the lodgers were transients. I had no television but I had bought a turntable stereo my last year of high school. All tenants shared a small bathroom down the hall with a tub and shower. I paid $10 a week for rent. Without a roommate I was now totally on my own, even though Pleasant Street was less than a mile from the house on Academy.

After I settled in, I sometimes invited a couple guys I'd known in high school over to listen to music. We'd buy a few quarts of Ballantine Ale in the big green bottles because it was cheaper. Talk eventually got around to what was happening in Vietnam. We had all registered with the local draft board over in Caribou when we turned eighteen. But my plan was to get back in college, get a student deferment, and not have to think of being drafted until I graduated. The war had seemed distant to us then, but it was gaining more attention with each passing month. *The Bangor Daily News*, that paper I'd delivered for over half my life, had been publishing the names of Maine soldiers killed in Vietnam. There had been nearly 60 already, including several from Aroostook County.

But mostly, on those nights in my room, we guys drank beer and listened to Johnny Cash or the Beach Boys. Word got back to me that my mother wasn't pleased to learn I was holed up in a bachelor pad. She had hoped the prodigal son might break. And yet, I *had* made my father proud in many ways. Now it was time to make *me* proud.

The aphids and ladybugs weren't nearly as congenial to work with as Professor Newman. For all his advanced education and serious study, he was as pleasant as they come. Sometimes he'd take me out to supper at one of the local restaurants. He often mentioned his wife and two children back in Ithaca, New York. I knew he missed them. When he learned that I was estranged from my own family, he took pity on me, especially since my girlfriend lived 35 miles away and I didn't own a vehicle. He had driven the family car up from New York, a later model Chevy. He encouraged me to use it to go visit Shirley on weekends. What a privilege to finally feel that independence without my mother riding shotgun with me to Van Buren.

Despite my rough beginning in Driver's Ed, I had actually become a competent driver. But I couldn't vouch for everyone else. One Saturday night as Shirley and I were driving out of the parking lot at the Gaiety Movie Theater, another car slammed into the front fender, leaving a sizeable dent. I was scared shitless. I was certain this meant the end of my job. Or, if I had to pay for the damages, it would mean the rest of my savings. My stomach was in knots as I picked up Professor Newman on Monday morning before work. When I confessed to him what had happened, he just shrugged it off. "It's no big deal, Ray," he said. "I have insurance. I'll get it fixed the next time I'm home." I was so impressed with that generosity of spirit. I had been raised to expect a harsher reaction. He even let me continue to use his car for the rest of the summer. It was a lesson in compassion I never forgot.

The summer that I moved out of my mother's house would go down as an all-time low in our relationship. I knew that if I went back for another year in college I'd need money for tuition. I had very little left in my savings account and student loans were nonexistent. Father Albert, still intent on turning me into a priest, was well aware that the Roman Catholic Diocese of Portland would not pay tuition for an aspiring priest who had flunked Bible Study and Biblical History. Without my knowing, he had gone around to the Presque Isle community asking a few prominent business people if they would help finance my second year. He even convinced them that I would work hard this time around and get respectable grades.

Had I known this in advance, I would have told him sooner than later. I would have *confessed*, so to speak. With this added pressure, it was time to take a stand. I could not, in good conscience, accept any money under the pretense that I was going to become a priest. I told Father Albert first, and then I broke the news to my mother. It was a good thing I had already moved out because a few more pots and pans went airborne.

Father Albert was more than disappointed. He had put himself on the line and now hated to go back to the folks he had convinced to help me. At least I was free of the guilt I'd been feeling all along. Or so I thought. A few days later my brother-in-law Tom, Del's husband, turned up at my boarding room to inform me that my mother was in the hospital with a gall bladder problem. He was another person not happy that I had moved out and was no longer contributing to the family. "Ray, you need to go visit your mother," was the advice he gave me. So I went. Mrs. Olore, the owner of Roma Café, was sitting in a chair by the bed when I arrived. When my mother started in again that I needed to move home and help her financially, our usual argument flared up. Mrs. Olore wasn't pleased to be in the middle of it. She told me to stop quarrelling with my mother since she was ill. I had a lot of respect for Mrs. Olore. I hadn't forgotten the big breakfasts she had cooked for me on cold winter mornings when Ginger and I were delivering newspapers. So I did the best thing I could. I left the hospital.

By the end of August, it was pretty clear that I wouldn't have enough money for my second year of college. That was if I managed to get accepted somewhere with my bad grades. I was trying to figure out my future when a letter decided it for me. I was still getting my mail at Academy Street. It was delivered to a metal box nailed near the front door. A couple days a week, I'd drive the Chevy over there on my lunch break and check the mailbox. I tried to plan my visits around times when no one would be at home to avoid confrontations. That's how estranged I felt from the family. Even aunts and uncles seemed to be on my mother's team. The only support I got was from Lisa, too young to take sides, and faithful old Ginger, who at least wagged his tail each time he saw me.

One Monday, as I was about to open the metal box near the front door, I saw Dana Bishop, our mailman, just turning up our walk. I went down the front steps to meet him. Mr. Bishop was the husband of my 4th grade teacher and one of the nicest men in town.

"I hate delivering letters like this one, Ray," he said. He then handed me an envelope. The sender was the Selective Service System, so I knew immediately what it was. A love letter from Uncle Sam. Enlistment had been slow after the United States declared war on Germany, in 1917, so Congress had quickly passed the Selective Service Act in order to raise an army to fight in Europe. Now they needed one to fight in Vietnam. I tore open the envelope and read the words that so many young American men were reading. In 1966 alone, almost 400,000 soldiers were drafted into military service, more than any other year during the Vietnam War. A couple million so far had received college deferments but I was no longer a member of that elite club.

The President of the United States was typed just above my name, *Raynold A. Gauvin* and the Academy Street address. No mistake there. It was for me all right. *You are hereby ordered for induction into the Armed Forces of the United States.* On October 18, I was to go to Bangor and turn myself over to the military. That's when I noticed the date stamped on the envelope: August 29, 1966. The previous day, a Sunday, marked the fifth anniversary of my father's death. It seemed like a lifetime had passed. I looked up at Mr. Bishop, who had served in World War II. He smiled sympathetically. He knew what I was feeling.

I had been more worried about my overall future than going to Vietnam. It wasn't that the war hadn't been in the limelight by this time. It held a regular spot on the nightly news, with Walter Cronkite explaining to us what was happening as best he could. American soldiers were dying, there was no doubt about it, and yet somehow our lives went on. Several thousand had been killed in the previous twelve months and four times as many South Vietnamese. We had started bombing North Vietnam the year before and the first major battle had been fought, the Battle of la Drang. More battles had followed by the time I got my draft papers. As the American public became aware of the casualties, thanks to television, a social unrest had started brewing. So many draft cards were being burned in protest that the U. S. Government had passed a law in 1965 making it a legal offense to destroy or mutilate one. That same year a Quaker set himself on fire in front of the Pentagon in protest, dying as a result of his burns.

When it became obvious that South Vietnam was losing the war to the Viet Cong, the U. S. had increased its number of troops in Southeast Asia. By early 1966, when I was eating fish & chips and flunking Biblical History back in Fredericton, nearly 200,000 American soldiers were already in Vietnam, and more were on the way. The objective, as far as the U. S. and South Vietnam were concerned, was to prevent a communist take-over. Most of the people I'd talked to about the war, including Professor Newman, wondered why it mattered to us Americans. That little country called Vietnam was a long way from Presque Isle, Maine. But it was the old domino theory. If South Vietnam fell, who would be next?

I folded the letter. The SSS emblem at the top was the Great Seal of the United States, an eagle facing to the left and holding a bundle of arrows in one claw, some laurel leaves in the other. The perpetual question after two hundred years was still the same one. *War* or *peace*? *Arrows* or *laurel leaves*? I shoved the letter back into the envelope.

"I'm going to enlist," I said to Mr. Bishop. It wasn't a spur of the moment decision. I'd been thinking of what I might do when that letter eventually arrived. Those of us who had registered for the draft were told that enlisting for three years meant we would not end up in the infantry. I didn't want to kill anyone. And I sure as hell didn't want anyone to kill *me*. Since my educational choices had pretty much dwindled by this time, I figured the army could teach me a new trade. I'd have something to fall back on once I was a civilian again. And I'd get to see some of the country, possibly the world.

Germany and Korea were my postings of choice. But I knew that enlisting was still no guarantee that I wouldn't end up in Vietnam.

"Good luck, son," Mr. Bishop told me. He patted my shoulder before he went on down the street, delivering that day's mail.

And so I had enlisted. We were expected at that time to choose our Military Occupational Specialty, what is known as our MOS. There are dozens of "jobs" in the military, but in the big picture they all fall basically into two categories: those that involve combat and those that support the troops in combat. I decided that the medical field would be a new challenge for me and possibly something I could rely on once I left the military. I chose X-ray technology, which seemed as far from the seminary as I could get. After nine weeks of basic training, I would begin my training as an X-ray technician.

When my work at the experimental farm ended in September, I thanked Professor Newman for his kindness to me. At the end of the month, I packed up all my stuff at Martin Manor and moved it back to the house on Academy Street. On October 17, I was ready to catch a bus out of Presque Isle which would take me to Bangor for my induction the following morning. Then, it would be on to Fort Dix for my basic training. Saying goodbye to Ginger was harder than saying goodbye to family since they were still giving me the cold shoulder. Ginger was twelve years old by that time and I wondered if I'd see him again. We'd been through a lot of snowstorms and downpours of rain together. I'd even taught him to carry papers in his mouth over to customers who got a kick out of seeing a dog delivering the news.

The morning I left, I walked over to the cemetery on North Main Street and visited Dad's grave. My mother drove me to the bus station.

We'd had a rough summer together and I knew she was still hurt over the decisions I'd made. In my memory of events, my mother cried that day. It's not easy to watch your oldest son go off into the world, especially if a part of that world is engaged in war.

There were only a dozen passengers on the bus. I sat in the last row of seats so I wouldn't have to talk to anyone. I wanted to think about my situation and what the future might hold. The bus route running south out of town was the same historic Route One that passed through Cyr Plantation, where my mother and her parents had been born, Van Buren, Shirley's hometown. On each side of the road were the rolling fields where I'd picked potatoes for local farmers, back in my growing up years. Next July the plants would be in full bloom again, as if the fields were filled with small purple stars. With the potato harvest now over, they were bare except for piles of brown stalks.

When Presque Isle disappeared behind me, I pulled Shirley's high school photo out of my wallet and stared down at it. She was now in Fall River, Massachusetts, in her first year of nursing college. She would be back in Van Buren for Christmas. I still wasn't sure if I would be coming home after basic training or not. If I did, I'd see Shirley then. My class ring was still on my finger, because she wasn't ready to go steady with any boy. That didn't bode well with me. But she was a respectable Catholic girl, another reason she never visited my rented room at Martin Manor. Kissing was as far as a good Catholic boy wanted to go anyway. It was almost a relief to be on that bus headed away from my old life. I was unsettled and unsure of my future. I knew that if I hadn't been drafted, with college out of the picture, I'd just be killing time with the guys, drinking Ballantine ale out of green quart bottles and listening to Johnny Cash.

Chapter 5

HELLO, UNCLE SAM

This is the State of the Union. But over it all—wealth, and promise, and expectation—lies our troubling awareness of American men at war tonight. How many men who listen to me tonight have served their Nation in other wars? How very many are not here to listen? The war in Vietnam is not like these other wars. Yet, finally, war is always the same. It is young men dying in the fullness of their promise. It is trying to kill a man that you do not even know well enough to hate. Therefore, to know war is to know that there is still madness in this world.

—PRESIDENT LYNDON JOHNSON

Annual Message to the Congress on the State of the Union,
January 12, 1966.

After passing my physical in Bangor and then swearing an oath to serve and protect my country, I got on a bus that took me to the next stage. I arrived for basic training in a drizzle of gray rain that kept up for days. Fort Dix, New Jersey, located less than twenty miles southeast of Trenton, had a history since World War I of preparing, organizing, and training troops for active service, as well as demobilizing them when their stint was up. It was named in honor of New Hampshire-born Major General John Dix, a veteran of the War of 1812, as well as the Civil War. Having talked to guys back in northern Maine who had been through basic training, I had a general idea of what to expect. For one thing, we were told we'd be in basic for eight weeks. But once we arrived, we were informed that there was a "zero week" reserved for getting us ready for training. That week didn't count.

Those first few days were spent getting our shots, processing our military records, and being issued uniforms and bedding. Unlike many other bases around the country that were still using old World War II barracks to house the men, Fort Dix had undergone a building program and the barracks were quite new. Instead of us all sleeping in one communal area, these rooms were designed for two-soldier occupancy. My roommate was a guy from nearby Trenton. I was assigned the bottom bunk and he got the top. We each had a metal closet and a wooden army chest for our belongings, fancy compared to the old barracks.

It didn't take long to realize the military was like a huge beehive that operated best with cooperation and production. Turning green-horn civilians into trained soldiers required a form of psychological overhaul in an environment that was new to us all. If we couldn't perform our assigned tasks during basic training—whether it was standing at attention, following a daily schedule, or just making our beds—then how could we be depended on in combat? If we ended up in a war zone, we knew that it didn't matter if we were cooks, office clerks, nurses, or X-ray technicians. If our compound was overrun, *everyone* was to take up arms to defend it. A good soldier who obeyed orders and followed the routine expected of him or her was one you could depend on when the bullets started flying. Or, as Colin Powell once put it, "the guy you take on a long patrol." When you accepted that basic theory, and knew you might end up in a war zone one day, you fell in line.

The first step was uniformity. We were instructed to leave our individuality at the barracks door. It was all about the larger picture now, what was good for the whole unit. One way to eliminate individuality was to eliminate diversity. Issuing us the same uniform and requiring our heads to be shaved was one way of making us look as much alike as possible. The shaved head wasn't so tough for those of us with a crew cut or a flat top. But it was 1966, and a lot of the guys were sporting an over-the-ears Beatles cut called the Arthur, or the pompadours of Elvis and Johnny Cash. The buzz line was a pretty solemn affair, like a silent rite of passage we were going through together, but where each of us had the space to let go of that final piece of personal style in his own way. My bunkmate had a classic waxed mop-top. When the shiny clumps hit the floor, I could almost hear a John Lennon voice say, "Goodbye Arthur."

Along with diversity went inhibition. We stripped down as a group for the showers, and stood side by side at urinals with no partitions in between for privacy. Having a bowel movement next to a fellow soldier who was also having a bowel movement is a learned art. You had to either pretend the other person wasn't there, or that he didn't care what your poop sounded like when it hit the can. The third option was to talk at the same time or make fun of the situation. Each of us seemed to have their own style of doing this and that fit reasonably well with each other. I was more comfortable with guys who exhibited a sense of privacy. Even shaved and stripped, modesty and pride still remained. But even those were to take knocks.

We were often referred to as fuck-ups, idiots, and numbskulls. We were dumber than stumps. Country boys tended to be in good shape since they came from rural areas where many local jobs required physical activity. But some soldiers were overweight or had never worked at a strenuous job. I often felt sorry for them, especially since the only way we could get to the mess hall was by way of the "horizontal ladder." This meant grabbing the rungs over our heads and "walking" fifteen bars with our hands, all the while hearing shouts in our ears of "Move it, private! Move it, fuck up! Move it, numbskull!" from the drill sergeant. Once there, we ate what was on our plates no matter that it wasn't our mother's cooking. One meat, one vegetable, one potato. Too often we ate "shit on a shingle," which was hamburger in a creamy sauce, served over a biscuit. I never seemed to get enough food and often felt hungry.

But mostly, the idea was to take a diverse group of young people from all different backgrounds, cultures, and religions, and turn them into a single team that could eat, work, sleep, and eventually go to war together. In many ways, I fit very well into army life. There was a subtle comfort in that routine of expectation, of always knowing pretty much how the day would unfold and what was required of me. As a kid from a big family with a bunch of part time jobs, I was used to structure. In some ways, as I proved during my time at university, I didn't quite yet know who I was without it.

A blow horn on a long telephone pole in the training area played reveille at 4 am to rouse us from our beds. The day was filled with calisthenics, tactical and survival skills, which included crawling under barbed wire, rappelling, marching, and shooting.

We were trained to use the M-14, which was the weapon of choice then for American soldiers. Evenings, we learned to clean our rifles and to take them apart and put them back together in less than a minute. We spit-shined our shoes and did our laundry. Some guys wrote letters home, but I wrote only to Shirley. I still felt an alienation from my family back in Maine. I didn't think much about it, though. We were exhausted by the time 9 pm rolled around and that same blow horn played taps to indicate lights out. Reveille came early. Having been that kid with a paper route for years, I was accustomed to rising before dawn; but thanks to our all-day training, I never woke up feeling rested.

I was only in basic training for two weeks before I had to have a painful wisdom tooth extracted. The dentist took the tooth out in the morning, and I was back in the field that afternoon. The weather all that time was all over the map, with mostly rain and fog. Just after Thanksgiving Day, we were hit with snow and ice pellets. Needless to say, inclement weather never stood in the way of our daily exercises. Temperatures would drop down low and then we'd get a warm day. I was used to that, too, from my newspaper route. The news must go out and a soldier must go on.

By mid-December, we had a few days in the 70s, and then the cold weather started in earnest. Maybe that's why I ended up in the hospital with pneumonia. I had to make up the exercises I missed by doing them during the evenings. There was no pampering, nor was it expected. No one was better than the next guy. If one of us didn't make his bed with exact precision, the drill sergeant stripped it and we tried again until we got it right. We even folded our t-shirts and socks the same way, and stored them in our chests the same way. The idea was not just consistency, but commonality.

We had a half hour each morning to wash, brush our teeth, shave, and eat our breakfast. During my first week at the base, the drill sergeant didn't approve of the way I was shaving. He was a black man, a well-decorated soldier from World War II and the Korean War. He was well over six feet tall and rugged, the kind of guy you don't want pissed off at you.

"That ain't how you shave, soldier!" he said to me, his face an inch from mine. "That's how old ladies shave!"

This was followed by a few expletives and adjectives to describe my limited IQ. I had no idea what I was doing wrong. My dad had passed away before he and I had gone through that rite of passage. The sergeant then grabbed the razor from my hand.

"You don't shave downward, numbskull! You shave upward, like this!" I felt instant pain, as if a fire were suddenly burning my face. That we were to do dry shaves, no shaving cream, was bad enough. But this was a shave from hell. It felt like he was taking flesh along with my facial hair. My face was on fire for a week until my skin was finally conditioned to the drill sergeant's idea of a good, close shave.

I got another lesson from the drill sergeant very early on. We had just finished doing forty push-ups and even though my arms were burning, I was proud that I was able to do that many so soon. A lot of the other soldiers were still struggling to build up their muscles. As I did my last push-up, the drill sergeant was leaning over me. I thought maybe he was going to praise my good work. I was wrong.

"Do another ten, soldier!" he screamed in my ear. Before I even thought about it, I blurted out, "But, Sir, I didn't do anything wrong." That was all it took. I thought his eyes were going to explode he was so angry.

"Do another twenty-five!" I think he then also commented on my overall worth as a human being, let alone a soldier in the United States Army. I'm surprised I got away with just more push-ups and not scrubbing all the latrines by myself with a tooth brush. I kept my mouth shut from then on. His job was to turn me into a soldier. My job was to accept it.

Before our basic training was up, about a dozen of us were ordered to report outside company headquarters. We did as we were told and stood in formation as we waited for the first sergeant to show up. Being singled out like that, and not knowing if it was a good thing or a bad thing, made the wait even more painful. When he finally appeared, we quickly saluted him.

"You have all qualified for OCS," he told us. "You can decline if that's your choice. Are there any questions?"

I could almost hear the thoughts of my fellow soldiers as we considered what this meant. Officer Candidate School. We had obviously been chosen because of our test scores. There were three categories from which candidates were selected, enlisted military, of which I was now one, college graduates, or civilians in other words, and direct commission, which included doctors, chaplains, and lawyers. Enlisted men, having already done some training, could pretty much count on making it through to graduation if selected for OCS. The success rate for guys like us was about 90 percent. One soldier raised his hand.

"Will we be going into infantry training?" he asked. The sergeant nodded. "That's the plan," he said.

My thoughts were still racing. This meant they would train us as officers to serve in combat in Vietnam. We'd graduate from OCS as second lieutenants. In the army, that was the entry rank for commissioned officers. A second lieutenant was the platoon leader, commanding anywhere from sixteen to forty-four men. He was at the head of his troops, the first one off a helicopter, and the last one on. He was also the first man at the head of his platoon as they went into battle. It wasn't the best job for someone without a good deal of combat experience in the field. But then, no soldier was safe in Vietnam. Radio operators and combat medics were a prize to enemy shooters because of the importance of their jobs. But hell, even grunts, those infantrymen who fought the war up close on the ground, had it bad. There were no guarantees in a war zone.

Only one soldier in our group raised his hand. The rest of us would take our chances as enlisted men. Maybe we'd end up in Vietnam, and maybe we wouldn't. Fifty-fifty looked pretty good when you considered the alternatives.

It was a couple of days before Christmas that our nine weeks were up. At our graduation ceremony, we looked in damn good shape. Guys who couldn't do more than a couple push-ups when they came in were doing a hundred. Boys who still had their baby fat and had been made fun of by the drill sergeants because they were overweight or pudgy were now young men in good physical form. The discipline had paid off. We were ready to move ahead and be assigned to what our chosen jobs in the army would be, our Military Occupational Specialty. Since my MOS was to be an X-ray technician I'd soon be on a plane to Fort Sam Houston, in Texas.

I decided not to go home first, but to spend the holidays on the base at Fort Dix. On Christmas Eve I used some of the meager salary I'd saved—my pay during all of basic training was $90.00—to telephone Shirley from a payphone and wish her a Merry Christmas. I could have gone up to Fall River, Massachusetts, where she was in nursing school, since it was only about six hours by bus. But she had already gone home to Maine for her school vacation. I was almost sorry that I hadn't done the same, especially since Shirley seemed a little uncertain about our relationship.

"Maybe we should take things more slowly, Ray," she said. Hell, if we went any slower, we'd stall. But I agreed with her since it was all I could do. I then called my mother. Just hearing her voice sent a wave of homesickness through me. She and my siblings were getting ready for Christmas Eve Mass at St. Mary's Church. I could imagine Academy Street decorated in festive lights and snow glistening along the sidewalks. Not that I missed shoveling it. Chapman Street would have put up all their Nativity scenes. Late shoppers would be packing the aisles at Zayre's, buying those electric knives, toasters, and Sunbeam mixers. And kids would be skating at the rink and on the river. There's nothing like a small New England city or town over the holidays. But I was still at Fort Dix by my own choosing.

On Christmas Day it started snowing and I didn't think it was ever going to stop. Eleven inches fell that one day. Before I got on a plane for Texas, a week later, another two and half feet had fallen. When I landed in San Antonio on the second of January, it was sunny and 66 degrees.

Fort Sam Houston sits less than four miles from the famous Alamo where Davy Crockett, James Bowie, and a couple hundred of their companions died at the hands of Santa Anna while defending the fort during the Texas Revolution. Considered the "Home of Army Medicine," as well as "Home of the Combat Medic," it included the Brooke Army Medical Center, where all army medical personnel trained, whether they were X-ray techs, radiologists, lab techs, nurses, or doctors. Fort Sam had housed nearly a thousand German POWS during World War II until nearby camps could be constructed. There was a more romantic side to the Fort's reputation, though; so many soldiers had met their future spouses while stationed there that San Antonio was jokingly referred to as the

"Mother-in-Law of the Army." Dwight D. Eisenhower became one of those soldiers, when he met and fell in love with Mamie Doud.

But I wasn't thinking romance when I got to Fort Sam and received orders that I was to undergo combat medic training. I had assumed I would be going to school right away to become an X-ray technician, and that would be my primary MOS. I found out later that *all* enlisted personnel who enrolled in the medical field were required to take combat medic training. That made "combat medic" my secondary MOS. It was a hell of an irony. I'd enlisted for three years to avoid combat. If I was sent to Vietnam as an X-ray tech and the army suddenly had a shortage of medics—and this was certainly likely—then I'd be called to the combat zone as a medic. Had I known this back at the recruiter's office in Presque Isle, I might have chosen a clerical MOS.

The eight weeks I had of combat medic training was divided between classroom instruction and field exercises. There were about twenty-six of us in my class. We learned to give shots, draw blood, insert IVs and perform CPR. It was difficult, but I enjoyed the challenge of learning how to treat certain injuries and deal with specific wounds.

The field exercises presented us with seemingly real scenarios based on events that could actually occur in the heat of battle. Using medical equipment, we treated superficial head and body wounds, whether from weaponry or burns. We were taught how to stop the flow of blood, keep airways open, treat seizures, perform tracheotomies, and use splints. We learned to identify the different types of shock and how to prevent or treat them, especially hypovolemic shock since it was the most common type in combat causalities. We even learned how to treat venereal disease. The whole time we took these classes and were educated about battlefield injuries, one word kept going through all our minds.

Vietnam.

It angered me daily, as I became more competent and skilled. The army had lied to me. Maybe it was the recruiter back in northern Maine who had deceived me. Maybe it was a priest, or even God. But *somebody*, somewhere along the line, had led me to believe that if I enlisted in the damned military for three years, I would avoid combat. Now here I was being trained for exactly that, and as a medic no less. Medics were all young men, mostly grunts with medical training. Those guys made second lieutenants seem invincible. And the Vietnam War couldn't seem to get enough of them.

On the other hand, there was a certain pride in knowing we were learning important techniques at Fort Sam. Just the year before, a study had been published by the National Academy of Sciences that became known as *The White Paper*. Its findings revealed that severely wounded soldiers on the battlefields in Vietnam had a higher survival rate than people who had been in serious car wrecks on California freeways. A major reason was that military medics were trained to perform critical advanced procedures such as airway management and fluid replacement, which could keep the victim alive as he was transported to a trauma facility. Another factor was the *speed* in which that patient was transported. It was a testament to our hard work and I tried to remember that. But I held on to the notion that I would be an X-ray technician, even if I did end up in the war zone.

By the time our eight weeks were up, I had been promoted to private second class. When we were tested on what we had learned, both in the classroom and in the field, I passed both tests easily. And then, there we all were, standing in formation as we awaited our next assignments. As names were called off, I felt my heart pounding. Some guys went to Korea, some to Germany, and some to Vietnam, as we had suspected. We all felt sorry for those guys. I wondered if any of them would come back.

Ray as a newly graduated X-ray technician at Fort Sam Houston.

We were all very aware that the war in Southeast Asia was escalating by the day. Finally, my name was called. I was assigned to X-ray school right there at Fort Sam! It was a few minutes before I could breathe normally again. In a matter of days I would be studying X-ray technology, exactly what I'd signed up for. It seemed a good omen for me, but I couldn't help think of the young medics, my fellow classmates, who would soon be landing in a war-torn country on the other side of the globe.

Those eighteen weeks at X-ray school marked my best experience in the military. Our classroom studies were courses in anatomy, physiology, and medical terminology. We also had onsite hospital training at Brooke Army Medical Center. We learned to take radiographs and how to shield patients from radiation. Although X-rays were turned over to a radiologist to analyze, we were taught how to read certain aspects, such as identifying the shades of grays, whites, and blacks of the area in question.

Thinking I might use this education once I left the army, I became fascinated with the history of radiology. In 1895, a German scientist named William Roentgen was first to discover X-rays while experimenting with electric currents. He noticed that a nearby florescent screen had begun to glow as the current passed through a tube. When he switched the current off, the glow disappeared. Because he didn't know which rays had caused the glow in the first place, he referred to them as "X-rays," or "unknown rays." One of the first he took was of his wife's left hand. In the image, he saw not only her bones but the wedding ring he had put on her finger. It was deemed a medical miracle that doctors could now see inside the human body without performing surgery.

Typically, the military responded immediately to these new findings. Mausers and the Martini-Henry rifle were then being used in European warfare, especially by the British Empire. This was modern weaponry with bullets that left small entry marks as they penetrated a soldier's body.

Just a year after Roentgen's discovery, X-rays were used on soldiers in the war between Italy and Abyssinia. American doctors used them in the Spanish-American War, in 1898. Portable X-ray equipment was soon being carried on the backs of mules and donkeys to makeshift hospitals in remote areas where battles were being waged.

But the hazards of this life-saving technology in the form of burns, blistering, and hair loss also began showing up. Some physicians denied the dangers of radiation, even after Thomas Edison's assistant died of skin cancer in 1904. And then Elizabeth Fleishman, a female pioneer, died a year later from the effects of her work. She was the first woman to die from radiation poisoning. It wasn't until the mid-1940s, and the aftermath of the Hiroshima bombing, that radiation dangers became undeniable.

One thing that caught my attention was a description of shoe-fitting fluoroscopes, or the "X-ray Shoe-Fitter," that many American stores had begun installing in the 1920s. Most stores banned them by the 1950s, but a few still had the device even into the 1970s. The box enabled customers to see the bones in their feet before they bought shoes. This would have been a popular 15-minute special back at Zayre's. I could imagine Mr. Waugh's high-pitched voice on the microphone excitedly telling shoppers to hurry over to the shoe department. Thank god the X-ray Shoe Fitter never reached northern Maine.

It was strenuous schooling, but there seemed to be more time now to socialize a little. When I could, I explored San Antonio. As a boy, I had greatly admired Davy Crockett and was finally able to visit the Alamo. Dad and I had been big fans of the 1950s television series in which Fess Parker starred as Davy. The later film and the hit song, "The Ballad of Davy Crockett," were so popular that kids started turning up at school wearing coonskin caps and fringed buckskin coats.

In my mind, the Alamo looked as it did back in 1836, a lonely fortress surrounded by the dusty plains of Texas. The battle cry "Remember the Alamo!" was a permanent testament to bravery. Even its name was historically impressive. The brochure I was given stated that it probably came from a nearby grove of cottonwood trees, which the Spanish called "álamo." By 1966, San Antonio had pretty much grown up around the fort. So my first and only visit was a bit disappointing. As I stood and stared at the barracks where the men had slept those nights they defended the fort before they died, I wondered what Davy Crockett would have thought of the Alamo now.

A couple times while I was at Fort Sam, some of us guys rented a car and drove down to Corpus Cristi for the weekend. We'd lie on the beach and watch the pretty girls stroll by. Eventually, the braver of us decided it was time to get a close-up look at Boys Town, down in Nuevo Laredo. It was just across the Mexican border from Laredo, about 150 miles away. We'd heard a lot about that place since we first arrived at Fort Sam. We were told that the booze was cheap and almost every smoky bar had a 6-piece Tejano band.

San Antonio might have been called the "Mother-in-Law of the Army," but Boys Town was well-known as "Sin City". While San Antonio had beautiful canals, parks, and restaurants, Boys Town had legal prostitutes and a river of tequila. It was a string of seedy brothels inside a walled compound on the dusty border between Texas and Mexico. It was contained inside a walled compound, sort of like a sleazy version of the Alamo. But soldiers and college boys were as common walking the streets down there as prostitutes, cowboys, gang members, and drunks.

Boys Town would become a marker in my life, albeit a hazy one. I had been gone from home now for six months. I had grown distant, during that isolation, from all that was familiar to me, everyone and everything back in northern Maine. This was what the military wanted, of course, and I could feel that change inside me. I had seen a lot more of the country, and met other guys from all over the States. I was a grown man of 21, and a soldier in the US Army. And yet, my girlfriend's letters had slowed to a trickle. I still hoped things would change once Shirley and I were together again, but Massachusetts was a long way from Texas. It was time to take my life up another notch, and Boys Town was the place to do it.

I even had enough money to make the trip. The army was paying me only $132.50 a month, but I picked up extra cash by giving plasma now and then. Plasma could be donated more often than blood, and it paid better. The downside of giving plasma was that once they separated it from your blood in a centrifuge, they put the blood back in you. But I did it a few times anyway, and now I was ready to spend my hard-earned dollars on something significant.

Four of us began planning a trip down to Nuevo Laredo. We needed a car worthy of such a symbolic trip and were willing to chip in on the rental fee. We wanted a Chevy Corvette like the Army Ranger drove on the TV show Route 66. It was the first TV drama to have a Vietnam veteran as a regular character. Man, that car was a beauty, but four soldiers couldn't fit into a Corvette with two seats. We needed a bigger car that was still cool. We talked of the trip all that week as we waited for Saturday. At the rental place, we immediately spotted the perfect car, a 1966 black Chevy Chevelle, shiny and new, and a convertible at that. We were all grinning as we waited for Bobby to sign the contract and be given the keys. We piled into the car, put the top down, and drove the desert highway south to the Mexican border. We had cranked the radio up loud so we could hear the music over the wind. *Black Is Black. Wild Thing. Sloop John B. Good Vibrations. Paint It Black. Nowhere Man. I Fought the Law. Secret Agent Man.*

When we arrived, we parked at the health clinic, which was next door to the police station. Bands were playing loudly in all the bars, and we started by pouring tequila into ourselves. As life got rosier, we flirted with the pretty girls in the bars. We danced and talked and drank some more. I wasn't much of a drinker, and that tequila hit me hard. Before I knew it, one of the girls took my hand and led me away as I laughed and wiggled by eyebrows at my friends. The fun had just begun.

I staggered down the stairs of a brothel sometime after midnight and out into one of the three narrow streets. When I painfully opened my eyes the next morning, I was sitting propped up against the building. My buddies were stretched out nearby, looking about as virtuous as I did.

Once we came to—even early in the morning there was a prostitute and her john everywhere you looked, not to mention that mysterious "health" clinic—the stark reality hit us. We could have been robbed or even killed long before any of us got drunk, let alone laid. Thank God the Chevy Chevelle was still where we had left it and hadn't been carried off in the night. But something looked different.

The hubcaps were gone.

The Chevelle was dust-covered, and now, written in that dust by the fingers of small Mexican children, were Spanish words we thankfully couldn't translate. Even with the language barrier, none of the words looked nice. I'd never seen upside down exclamation points in my life. Our heads aching, we slowly unlocked the doors and got in. Bobby sat for a time behind the wheel before he started the engine. We left the top up since wind doesn't go well with a hangover. Every bump on the road back to the border made my head hurt more.

Once I recovered from my visit to Boys Town, I was ready for more exploration. Yes, I had a girlfriend back at her safe Catholic nursing school. But I was still not certain where Shirley's head was when it came to our relations. She had never asked me to be faithful to her. Given the circumstances, I didn't feel I had the right to ask that of her either. In one letter she told me that her sister, Diane, had enlisted in the military and was training as a lab tech at Fort Sam. She was pretty, and fun-loving, very different from Shirley, who tended to view life in a more serious vein. I even speculated on whether or not I'd focused on the wrong sister.

I let one of my buddies set up a blind date for me with a girl in the Women's Army Corps who was training at Fort Sam. I might have survived Sin City, but I still wasn't very experienced in dating. This girl was the daughter of a Baptist minister, but you wouldn't know it by how she was dressed, in a short skirt and tall boots. She spent most of our date telling me how much she wanted to get married and have babies. I just nodded as I ate pizza and sipped my beer.

When my training ended and I graduated from X-ray school, I was assigned to do my residency at Madigan Army Medical Center up at Fort Lewis, Washington. Fort Lewis was located on a sprawling acreage just south of Tacoma. It was named in honor of Meriwether Lewis who had trekked to the mouth of the nearby Columbia River with Sacajawea and William Clark, in 1805. Standing on the riverbank, Lewis had been the first settler to view the Pacific Ocean. Madigan was a debarkation hospital for the ports of Seattle, Tacoma and Portland, Oregon, for soldiers wounded in combat and coming home from the front lines.

At Fort Lewis, I was finally able to put into practice what I'd learned in Xray school. Now I would be working with real patients, all military personnel and their families, in an actual X-ray situation. It was challenging as we'd trained at Fort Sam for only eighteen weeks. In civilian life, an X-ray tech would need a year of instruction before being qualified. Most of the X-ray techs in 1966 were men. Lab techs tended to be mostly women.

I learned a lot at Fort Lewis and Madigan Hospital. And yet, one incident stands out above all others. One day, a woman in her 50s came in to be X-rayed. She was a beautiful, blue-eyed brunette with a great body, and you could tell right away she worked out. The problem was a pain in her left shoulder she'd incurred during a game of tennis. I assumed that she and her friends played a lot of tennis at the local country club. All I knew for certain is that she was tall, with great legs. Everything about her was well-groomed, her hair perfect, her fingernails manicured.

I gave her a johnny gown and told her that she would need to remove her bra since it would have metal hooks or clasps. I also reminded her to remove her jewelry, no easy task since she wore rings, a watch, bracelets, earrings, and a necklace. I remember wondering how much plasma I'd have to give to buy it all. She took the johnny and smiled, showing perfect white teeth. When I returned a few minutes later, and knocked on the door, she told me to come in.

When I stepped into the room, I stopped in my tracks. She was stark naked on my X-ray table. The johnny was still neatly folded at her feet. They hadn't warned me about *this* during my training at Fort Sam. My mouth dropped open.

Finally recovering, I said, "Ma'am, I'm going to leave the room again. I'll need you to please put on the gown I gave you."

I waited outside the door, still stunned. "Even with a sore shoulder?" I kept thinking. After a few minutes had passed, I knocked loudly. When I went back in, she was wearing the johnny. And on her face was that playful smile. She knew exactly what she was doing. Either I would have been game and taken her up on the offer, or I would have left the room. I wondered about her other medical appointments over the years. How many times had a young doctor or technician locked the door and stayed?

"It'll be about an hour for me to develop the film," I said to her, once I'd finished taking the X-rays.

"Then I'll come back in an hour," she replied, smiling. "I don't like waiting."

In those days, we did the developments manually in a darkroom, usually taking 45 minutes to an hour. I finished the development and couldn't see anything wrong with her shoulder. But that was up to the radiologist to conclude. When I went out to the waiting room to give her the envelope with her X-rays, a few other patients were sitting in chairs. Next to my frisky patient sat a brigadier general with that 1-star blazing on his shoulder patches. I immediately saluted him.

"Honey," she said to the general, "this is the young man who took my Xrays. He was very professional."

She smiled that perfect smile that had probably made some dentist a lot of money.

I understood then that she was a bored military wife who got her kicks out of seducing young soldiers. Perhaps she did it as revenge on her husband, the lower the rank, the greater the revenge. I tried not to think of what would have happened to me had I accepted her offer and "General Honey" had opened the door on us. I'd probably still be in some lonely stockade at Fort Lewis, fighting off rats and rattling my chains.

When my sixteen weeks were up at Fort Lewis, I was promoted to private first class. I then received orders to report to Fort Belvoir,

Virginia, and the 13th Field Hospital. I was still not headed to Southeast Asia, but the unit was training and holding future placements for Korea, Germany, and Vietnam. I knew I was getting closer to being deployed to the war zone. So, before I reported to the base, I flew back to Presque Isle. My sister Diane was getting married on October 14, so it was a good time for me to go home. I'd been gone for a year. I wasn't the young man who had left on the bus that day twelve months earlier, still fresh from counting aphids. It was time to start the healing in the Gauvin family. At least I hoped it was time.

Again, the potato fields were brown with dead stalks left from the recent harvest. The leaves were still at their peak colors, the yellow of aspen and oak, the scarlet of maple, and the golden yellow of birch. Diane's future husband, Tom, picked me up at the Presque Isle airport. He was a good choice for my sister, a boy raised by his grandparents after his own parents were killed in an automobile accident. I had been asked to be best man at the wedding, but didn't know if I'd get a furlough home when they'd set the date. I was pleased when I made it.

As we drove up to the house on Academy Street, I knew I was coming home more mature and wiser than when I'd left. We had all matured in the year I'd been gone, and in different ways. Now Diane, who was just fourteen years old when our father died, was getting married. There was new siding on the house and even a new roof. Dad would have been pleased. He had felt proud the day we had moved from the small house on Chapman Street, away from the rattling trains and up to "the hill." Ginger was lying near the front door. He lifted his head when he saw me coming up the porch steps. I knelt down and put my arm around his neck. He was getting on in years when I had left, and now he seemed even thinner than I remembered.

"Hey, boy," I said. "How you been?"

His tail wagged immediately, greeting me in that kind way that faithful dogs know so well. I was his oldest friend. I had to wonder how many newspapers we'd delivered as a team, come snow, rain or sunshine.

I closed the front door quietly behind me and tossed my duffel bag on the sofa. Then I went to the kitchen to find my mother. Without speaking a word, the first thing we did was embrace. I hoped she was glad to see me. It certainly felt good to be home. Lisa came running to jump into my arms. She was six years old by now and a sweet little girl, happy to see her big brother again. Everyone was in a good mood and excitement was in the air. Mom had cooked a lot of the food I loved. On the counter I saw a lemon meringue pie, still my favorite, and there was the heart-shaped cake that had celebrated so many of my sister Del's birthdays. The focus was now on the upcoming wedding and that made it easier for us to interact. If there were still cracks, they were covered up well.

After the hellos and hugs were over, I slipped past the sun room where Dad's office used to be. A year or so after his death, Mom had turned it into a dining room for the family, but the floors were the same ones he had sanded and varnished by hand. I went downstairs to the basement and stood in the doorway of his workshop. His tools were still hanging from hooks on the wall. There was that familiar feel to the place, a smell almost, maybe Old Spice aftershave and the slight trace of cigarette smoke. It was as if the memories of my father and me working on model trains were still there. I thought of all the times we'd raided the dump for discarded junk. In this workshop, we had turned that junk into treasures.

The last day my father was alive, he had tied the bow on Diane's blue dress and told her how pretty she was. Maybe that was something she could remember as she walked down the aisle, another man giving her away. *Something borrowed, something blue.* He would have just turned forty-nine years old. But with his sudden disappearance, Hector Gauvin's family had done what human beings have always done. We had mourned, and then we had moved on in our lives without him.

It was time now to think ahead to the future and Diane's big day. Gilman would be home for the wedding. He was attending the

University of Maine down in Orono. I had no doubt that he was acing all of his courses with very little study. Gary was a sophomore in high school. I figured this made Mom's load a lot easier with just two children to worry about. The apartments were still doing well, as she had told me when I inquired. She was proud to have built up her own credit in Presque Isle, something most married women didn't have in those days. Always a hard worker, Mom was still part-time at Roma Café. She had even opened a savings account. There was a self-confidence in her now that hadn't been there before.

After supper that night I went upstairs to peer into my old bedroom. There was the desk that had gotten me through high school, all those notes I'd carved on its top. I hoped Gary was using it now. I closed the door. Since Gary had moved into my bedroom with Gilman after I left for school in Fredericton, it hadn't been my room for a couple of years. When it came time for us to turn in, Mom pulled the living room sofa out into a makeshift bed. It was only right that Gilman sleep upstairs when he got home from college. I even preferred the solitude downstairs. And after a year of army cots, I didn't mind the sofa at all. Mom found sheets, blankets, and a pillow from the linen closet and made the bed up for me.

I snapped off the lamp and settled in for the night. I was exhausted from the long flight. I had planned on calling Shirley to let her know I arrived safely. I'd do it the next day. For now, I just wanted to lie on the sofa in that house where I'd come of age, the last place I'd seen my father. Ginger had slumped down on the floor next to the sofa so I rested my hand on his back. There were the usual creaks and groans in the house that I remembered from the early years. Water gushed through the pipes. I heard Lisa tell my mother goodnight and then a bedroom door close. Upstairs, Gary and Gilman laughed over some joke. There were footfalls on the stairs as someone came down to the kitchen for a glass of water. Then the house fell into silence. I drifted off to sleep, comforted by the familiar ghosts of my past.

Chapter 6

TRANSITIONS

D iane's big day had gone off perfectly even though the wedding had started a half hour late. It seems the ring-bearer, a kid from a nearby town, was being driven to the wedding by his parents. A few miles from the church, their car had a flat tire. I didn't mind the delay since my brother and I had been out partying the night before. It was supposed to be the typical bachelor party, but the future groom declined to come with us. Tom wanted to spend that last evening of his bachelorhood with my sister, his future wife. You can't argue with a genuine guy like that. I was happy that Diane had found the perfect mate for her. It also made me wonder about my own future. I was eager to see Shirley again, face to face.

Two weeks after my sister's wedding, I was checking in at the 13th Field Hospital. Already it seemed as if my first visit home in a year had been a dream. I was back in military mode the instant I stepped onto the base. There's a good reason behind not letting soldiers go on leave for too many days. The military doesn't want them to forget that they are no longer an individual, but part of a well-organized machine.

The public resentment toward the war was intensifying. A few days after my arrival at Fort Belvoir, on October 21, a crowd of nearly 100,000 had gathered in the nation's capital to voice their opposition to America's involvement in the war. About half of them then marched to the Pentagon, 35,000 to 50,000 strong, carrying signs that demanded an end to the conflict. Military police, federal marshals, and Army troops with rifles surrounded the Pentagon. I was one of the troops. From my station on the roof of the Pentagon, I paced as I watched demonstrators approach the troops. Some demonstrators were photographed putting flowers into the barrels of the rifles. It was obvious from a poll taken a few months earlier that the American public was more opposed to the war now than for it. Over 20,000 soldiers had died in Vietnam, and that was just the Americans. For those of us caught in the crosshairs, there wasn't much we could do but serve our time. At the end of my duty, I thanked God that I had not had to use my weapon on any of my countrymen.

The military is all about preparing soldiers not just to fight a war, but to deal with its aftermath, the wounded first and the dead afterwards. At Fort Belvoir we learned how to set up a field hospital in a combat zone. For much of history, any soldier who sustained wounds during a battle would be left to lie where he fell as the battle raged on. It was a physician in Napoleon's army who first organized a unit of litter-bearers, who were selected to carry the wounded from the battlefield. These were usually soldiers who were considered the worst of the lot, incompetent and therefore dispensable. After casualties became so high during the American Civil War, especially at the Second Battle of Bull Run, near Manassas, and a month later at Antietam, General George McClellan requested Dr. Jonathan Letterman to do what he could to fix the problem. Antietam would mark the bloodiest day in American warfare, with almost 23,000 soldiers dead or wounded.

Many of those who died might have lived, had they not lain suffering for hours, even days on the battlefield. Letterman, who was the medical director of the Army of the Potomac, took up the challenge and amazingly redesigned the army medical corps. Near the battlefronts, he set up hospitals anywhere he could find enough space, a public hall, a private home, even churches and schools. He quickly devised the three-tiered evacuation system, which is still in effect today: (1) field dressing and aid stations near the battlefield (2) field hospitals further away from the battle, such as in private homes, churches, and even barns, and (3) large hospitals at a safe distance from the front lines.

Dr. Letterman didn't stop there. Aware that the quicker these soldiers were treated, the better their chances of survival, he wanted them off the battlefield as soon as possible. Remembering how Napoleon's army had used its litter-bearers, which the British had also started doing during the Crimean War, he trained corpsmen and equipped them with what they needed to carry the wounded to the field aid stations. All of this history that I was learning, which had happened over a hundred years earlier, had taken place very close by. The battles of Bull Run had been fought in August of 1862, just 25 miles from Fort Belvoir. The battle of Fredericksburg, in December of that same year, was where Letterman's three-tier evacuation plan had first been tested. And *that* battleground was only 30 miles away.

Thanks to Dr. Letterman, we were learning how to set up a field hospital in a portable tent, rather than a church, or barn, or some-one's house. We did it on a daily basis. We drove everywhere in an old army cargo truck called a deuce-and-a-half, since it weighed a ton and a half. We packed up all of our equipment, drove the rat-tling truck to where the tent was to be set up, unpacked everything, assembled the field hospital, then tore it all apart, packed the supplies onto the truck, and rattled back to the barracks. The next day we repeated the same exercise. It got so boring that I became a coffee drinker, something I'd never been. The tent itself was big enough for about 20 cots to be set up inside, rather like a mini-hospital. The television-viewing public saw an older version of this on the hit series M.A.S.H.—*mobile army surgical hospital.*

We laid out supplies inside the tent, like medical kits, syringes, tourniquets, and splints. We set up equipment that doctors and nurses would need to treat burns, shock, head wounds, seizures, and gunshot wounds. They could draw blood, set up IVs, and perform C.P.R. or tracheotomies, anything that was required to save a soldier's life. In real situations, those seriously injured would be airlifted by helicopter to a real hospital, usually in Cam Rahn Bay, or Japan. The ones with minor wounds would be treated and sent back to the fighting. There were no "front lines" in the Vietnam War, as in previous wars. The enemy could be anywhere, even slipping onto American military bases at night to toss a grenade or open fire.

I might have been bored, but I was paying close attention to details. One minute I was certain I wouldn't be sent to Vietnam. The next minute I wasn't. There was a dark feeling hanging over me that I couldn't explain, a kind of premonition that grew stronger each day. What if I *was* sent to Vietnam, and as a combat medic, not an X-ray technician? Never were medics more needed or used more effectively than in Southeast Asia during the war. I'd received combat medic training at Fort Sam, after all. It was my secondary MOS. Now, at Fort Belvoir, we were hearing about how indispensable medics were. They were usually young soldiers, most of them barely twenty years old. I was an old man having just turned twenty-two.

Combat medics didn't just carry medical supplies. They also carried grenades and M-16s. They fought right along with the other soldiers when necessary. They'd even become radio operators in a pinch. They were an incredibly valuable member of any platoon. In Vietnam, with helicopters serving as air ambulances, an injured soldier's chance of survival once he was *en route* to a field hospital greatly increased. He could be moved quickly from the scene of battle and air-vac'd. Sometimes, the medic who first treated him climbed onto the helicopter to continue working on him until they reached the field hospital and doctors and nurses took over. I respected the hell out of combat medics. But no way did I want to become one.

Searching in the jungles for Viet Cong

While we wondered where we would be headed, we nonetheless had time to explore the area and have some fun. I was becoming less shy and more social. We would often go up to nearby Georgetown, known for its nice restaurants and pubs. The guys and I liked to mingle with the pretty girls from Georgetown University who were often in the local bars and taverns. All the civilian guys had long hair, certainly longer than our buzz cuts. It was obvious that we were military when we walked in the door, even without our uniforms. The girls still danced with us even though we got brooding looks from the other men.

There were a lot of high-rise apartment buildings in the D.C. area where many of the government workers lived, employees from the State Department or the Pentagon. A couple times we selected a high-rise at random and just strolled inside as if we lived there.

There was almost no security. We walked the halls, going from door to door listening for a stereo playing "Mrs. Robinson," or "Sittin' on the Dock of the Bay," or "Midnight Confessions." When we found a party, we opened the door and walked in as if we were invited. Before we left, we'd have plenty of quickly-scrawled phone numbers from pretty girls. None of them were ever accurate. It was all harmless fun, and it eased the tension of what lay ahead for us.

One night it got a little shaky. It was quite late and we were on our way back from a nightclub. For some reason, the driver of the vehicle decided to drive onto the base using the back gate. Suddenly, there in the road ahead, were a lot of flashing lights and what looked like cruisers. It was the military police looking for a soldier who had just robbed a grocery store. We were asked to get out of our vehicle and stand spread-eagle against it. It was a case of very bad luck that I fit the description, my height, hair-color and dark-framed eye glasses. I spent that night in the brig with another guy who was sound asleep on one of the four cots. He looked like he had ended up on the wrong side of a fistfight. He had a cut over his eye and his shirt was ripped. When I was released early the next morning after the true culprit was arrested, my roommate was still snoring.

Always looking for a way to make a few extra bucks, I got a part-time job as an X- ray tech in the emergency room of a local clinic. This was okay with the military. I'd been promoted to E-4 by then, or non-commissioned officer rank. Since we were no longer in training, an off-base job like that was allowed. It was my opportunity to work with the general public for the first time. There were the usual medical problems you'd expect, from broken arms to slipped discs and sprained fingers.

A financial opportunity I discovered on the base, however, earned me the really good bucks, although it might be considered innocent racketeering. It had to do with KP duty, what is known as Kitchen Police or Kitchen Patrol. KP was any chore given to junior enlisted personnel by the kitchen staff. Hollywood movies tended to depict

KP duty as a minor punishment to soldiers, and it sometimes was. But mostly it was a necessary chore that needed doing in order for the mess crew to feed all those hungry men. No one made KP duty more famous than the lazy and unlucky Beetle Bailey, that comic strip character who seemed eternally doomed to peeling potatoes, and who once told Sergeant Snorkel he would peel faster if he were "paid by the potato."

In reality, KP included washing dirty dishes, sweeping and mopping floors, scrubbing pots and pans, wiping down the tables, and serving food on the chow line. Some soldiers really didn't mind KP and others actually liked it. But a whole lot of the guys hated it with a passion. Who wanted to sit on a stool and stare at 500 pounds of potatoes that were waiting to be peeled? Those were the guys I focused on, the KP-haters. I soon had a successful business strategy in place. Most haters were willing to pay fifteen bucks to get shed of washing tons of dirty dishes or mopping floors. So I became a broker. I matched them to the guys who didn't mind KP and who were willing to take the duty themselves. I paid the KP-lovers a cool ten bucks, which was a nice piece of change considering what the army was paying them. And I kept five bucks as my commission. It was a business model in which everyone left the stage happy. I hadn't lost those entrepreneurial chops I'd developed as a kid after all. My greatest concern during my brokering days was getting caught by my commander, a female nurse who I greatly liked and respected.

In basic training at Fort Dix I had learned to use the M-14. But at Fort Belvoir we were now expected to qualify with the M-16. Among the many problems with the M-14 during battle was that soldiers couldn't carry enough ammunition to maintain superiority over the AK-47, the weapon of choice used by the Viet Cong and the North Vietnamese Army, and supplied to them by both Russia and China.

The AK-47 was lightweight compared to the M-14s. It was also known to be reliable in combat, with its rapid- fire capability. Spitting out thirty 7.62 mm bullets in fast succession, like a machine gun, meant that the enemy didn't have to be the best shot in town. He was likely to hit his target anyway. The AK-47 also adapted better to the tropical climate of Vietnam, with its scorching sun, high humidity, and frequent rainfall. In early 1963, when reports of the M-14's inadequacy had reached Robert McNamara, the Secretary of Defense, he ordered a halt to its production.

The military started using the M-16 the next year, in 1964. It soon became the gun deployed with American soldiers to the jungles of Vietnam. By 1965, almost 60,000 of them were had been delivered to the troops there. But there were serious problems, one being that the weapons didn't come with proper cleaning kits or adequate instructions. The manufacturer, Colt, insisted the gun was self-cleaning. It wasn't. In that moist climate, the barrels often corroded. The worst problem of all was "failure to extract," which meant that the spent cartridge case stayed lodged in the chamber after the weapon was fired. Still hoping to hell and back that I wouldn't end up as a combat medic, I nonetheless qualified as an expert on the M-16 while at Fort Belvoir.

The year 1968 had begun with such calamity that it would go on the textbooks as one of the most explosive and turbulent years in our country's history. The unrest actually started on the other side of the globe in the pre-dawn hours of the Vietnamese lunar new year, *Tet Nguyen Dan*, which would become known to the American public as *Tet*. But its repercussions were soon felt in the United States when newscasts began reporting what had happened, an all-out attack on American forces in Vietnam and our allies, the ARVN, Army of the Republic of Vietnam.

Under the command of General William Westmoreland, the Army Chief of Staff, we learned from daily briefings how high the enemy body count was. As a matter of fact, Westmoreland had said in a *Time* magazine interview in the autumn of 1967 that he wished the Communists *would* make a move. "I hope they try something," he said, "because we're looking for a fight." They got it when the

North Vietnamese forces ignored what had previously been an informal truce during the most important holiday on their calendar.

In our minds it was inconceivable that a small agricultural country like Vietnam could possibly threaten the greatest military force in the world. It's been recorded that the message the North Vietnamese troops, the People's Army of Vietnam (PAVN) received from Hanoi, on the night their attacks began, was "Crack the sky, shake the Earth." After months of secret planning and storing up tons of weapons and supplies sent courtesy of China and Russia, almost 200,000 North Vietnamese troops made their way south, using the Ho Chi Minh trail. They were armed with grenade launchers and new AK-47 assault rifles. The plan was to carry out surprise attacks against a hundred or more cities and villages in South Vietnam where military and civilian centers were positioned.

They had already launched an attack over a week earlier on Khe Sanh, possibly as a diversion to draw our military's attention away from the more populated areas.

Now they were putting into action what would become known to the world as Phase I of the Tet Offensive. On January 30, with the holiday about to begin, several areas in Saigon were attacked, including the U.S. Embassy. By the time the enemy was subdued at the embassy, five American personnel were killed. The next day, allied forces near the city of Hue, north of the Perfume River, were bombarded by rockets and mortars, and then two battalions of the enemy attacked. The fighting at Hue would go on for 25 days and mark one of the bloodiest and longest battles of the Vietnam War.

Although the Allies could declare a victory, the city was destroyed in the process and a few thousand civilians were killed, over half of them executed by the Viet Cong and PAVN. We lost 668 American soldiers in that battle. Almost 4,000 were wounded. I got news from home that one of my classmates at Presque Isle High had been in the fighting at Hue and miraculously was among the survivors. With the media now covering the fighting as never before, the reality was soon turning up on American television sets. The war had certainly escalated. It had become obvious that we'd miscalculated the fighting machine in that little "backward" nation.

What else had escalated was the simmering social and political climate in the United States. The depressing news now coming back from Vietnam seemed to comingle with our own unrest. A month earlier, on April 4, Martin Luther King, Jr. had been shot and killed as he stood on the balcony of his Memphis motel room. Almost immediately the country exploded in riots so violent that after a month almost 50 people would be dead. President Lyndon Johnson called for a day of national mourning, but it did little good. Cities like Chicago, Baltimore, and nearby Washington D.C. seemed on the verge of self-destruction as racial tensions between whites and blacks raged out of control. And yet, that same month, and thanks to the hard work and dreams of Martin Luther King, the Civil Rights Act of 1968 was passed. King's death had been the impetus for Lyndon Johnson's request that the bill go forward. Yet it seemed too little too late in the big picture. As I and my fellow soldiers waited at Fort Belvoir for our next orders, we wondered if the whole damn world had gone to hell.

I finally received orders to my next assignment in early May. I was called to the captain's office and she handed me the papers. I stared hard at the words, trying to decipher the military's love of codes and acronyms, which are used more to convey information to the Finance Office and Human Services Department than to the soldier receiving them. *GAUVIN, RONALD A RA11599821.* That was my serial number, following the letters RA, for *Regular Army*, which would distinguish me from Army Reserve and National Guard, and also Army of the United States, which represented drafted soldiers.

The officer who typed the orders had misspelled my first name. Regardless, I was to report to Fort Dix, NJ *for fur asg to USA WDMET.* This meant "for further assignment to USA WDMET." The address was APO SF 96307. That didn't tell me anything. All the APO numbers to locations during the Vietnam War began with 9 and 6, whether you were going to Korea, Cambodia, Thailand, the Philippines, or even Australia. Then my eyes skimmed down to this line: *Indiv will arr in Viet Nam wearing khaki trousers and short sleeve khaki shirt.*

"Gauvin, I guess it's Vietnam," the captain said. "Tan Son Nhut, Saigon." There seemed to be a genuine sadness in the way she said it. There was certainly sadness in how I felt about it.

"Yes, Captain," I said.

Who do you argue with? The Pentagon? God? Maybe even the devil? You argue with *no one* when you belong to Uncle Sam. I had enlisted, after all. I had been damn well-trained by the military, and at its expense. I would do what I had to do. But what the hell was WDMET? Would I be assigned to a medical unit? And why, as I would soon learn, was I the only soldier in my unit at Fort Belvoir chosen for it? I saluted the captain, and she returned my salute. Then I spun on my heel and left her office.

It was mid-May in Northern Maine when I arrived home on leave. The frost was gone from the ground and the potato farmers were readying their fields for planting. As my plane descended, I could see tiny tractors pulling harrows to break up the soil. Clouds of brown dust rose up in their wakes.

Despite the good rapport we had on my last visit, I still felt like an outsider in the Academy St. house. It seemed to me that we were all changing, all going in different directions. When it came time to leave, I drove to St. Mary's Cemetery where my father was buried. There was a lilac bush near the cemetery gate, freshly bloomed. I broke off a branch and carried it with me as I found his grave. I realized that the man standing at my father's gravesite wasn't the teenager who stood there seven years earlier. We were now all different, my mother, my sisters, my brothers and me. In truth, the only person who had remained exactly the same was my father, at least in our memory of him. I put the branch of lilacs on his grave. I hoped the day would come when I could visit him again.

Before I reported to Fort Dix, I made arrangements to see Shirley. She was just finishing her second year of nursing school. I felt terrible that I had been unable to spend quality time with her for two years. But sentimentality has little place in the military, especially in wartime. Shirley agreed to meet me in Boston, a distance of some fifty miles. I had thought about this get-together for weeks and not just because I was going to Vietnam. That may have been a subconscious part of it. The conscious part was that it would be nice to belong to someone. For the last year and a half, I had been owned by the damn army. I'd slept on cots and bunk beds. I'd eaten in mess halls surrounded by the noise of other soldiers. I'd taken orders from my superiors. I wasn't a kid anymore. A lot of guys my age were married and some were already fathers, with a starter home and a white picket fence. If I was lucky, I'd be back from Vietnam in a year. Shirley would be done with school and ready for a career herself. We both wanted to settle down in northern Maine. It was time to put the subject on the table.

I waited for her at the bus station, as we'd planned. It was a gray and cloudy day, with a fine mist of rain. She was wearing a tan trench coat and had a blue scarf wrapped around her neck. I gave her a tight hug. I think I lifted her into the air and twirled her around. I remember her laughing. Her hair was shorter than when I'd seen her last. She had always worn it down to her shoulders, but now it was just below her ear. It was a more sophisticated look, as if proof that she'd been away from her family for two years and was older and wiser. I knew the feeling. I'd done the same thing. We had the whole afternoon and evening to spend together. I didn't have to report to Fort Dix until the next day at noon. I could catch a flight early the next morning.

Shirley suggested we visit a couple of the most historic sites and then find a little café for lunch. But I didn't want to go to the usual tourist attractions like Bunker Hill or the Old North Church. At Bunker Hill the British had won. Yet they lost so many men, including 34 commissioned officers, that the number of casualties made it appear more like a defeat. A *pyrrhic victory, it's called.* It was a battle where Americans would first become familiar with the phrase, "Don't fire until you see the whites of their eyes." And the Old North Church had its own memories of war, when those two lanterns had hung in the steeple. We had studied the Longfellow poem in school. "One if by land, two if by sea." I wanted to forget about battles, about soldiers and drummer boys dying.

I convinced Shirley that we should go to a quiet café instead, sit over a glass of soda and a beer. Catch up on our lives. There was only so much we could convey in those letters and phone calls over the many months that had passed. She had wanted to go more slowly she had told me the Christmas Eve I'd phoned her from Fort Dix. Maybe it was time to speed things up again. We had shared so many good times back in northern Maine. I wanted to talk about a little house one day, like the one I'd grown up in on Chapman Street. A couple of kids. A good loyal dog like Ginger. We could think of being tourists another day. The catching up didn't take long. After some chit-chat about my stint at Fort Belvoir, she told me about the surprise engagement party she and her friends were planning for one of their classmates. Finally, nervous, I brought up the subject of our future together.

"I'll be back from Vietnam in a year," I told her. "We've been seeing each other for a long time, Shirley. Maybe we should think about a life together." I still wasn't sure if I might propose. I figured it would all depend on her.

She didn't respond right away. She hadn't seemed all that concerned that I was going to Vietnam, no more than a good friend might be. There was an aloofness in her attitude toward me from the moment I'd met her at the bus station. I had chalked it up to that newly acquired sophistication. Sure, she had grown beyond the

Shirley I knew. I had grown, too. I assumed that the distance between us in miles over the past months had caused the gulf between us now. And it would close again once I got back from Vietnam.

It wouldn't be the first time in my life I was dead wrong.

"I wanted to tell you this in person," Shirley said. "I'm just not the girl for you, Ray. I tried to tell you sooner. I just didn't want to hurt you."

She had picked a damned poor time to tell me now. I didn't know how to respond. But it suddenly made sense. I hadn't seen her in person since I'd gotten my draft notice. I'd called her after basic training and offered to take a bus up to Fall River, but she was going home for the holidays. The two times I had been home on leave, she had to stay on campus in Fall River and study. She *had* tried to tell me. *Maybe we should take things more slowly, Ray.* Looking back over the months, she had started signing her letters *Love, Shirl*. She probably did that every time she wrote to one of her friends. That's what I really was, if I admitted the truth. I was a friend.

"I really can't stay long," Shirley said then. "We've got finals next week. I should get back."

I paid our bill and then helped her on with her coat.

"I'll walk you back to the bus station," I said, and she nodded. She did her best to cheer me up as we walked, pointing out things along the sidewalk, a building, a vendor, a store window, anything to direct attention away from the reality of that moment.

"Good luck, Ray," she said. "Take care of yourself over there." I hugged her goodbye and then watched as she disappeared inside the station. She didn't turn to look back. But I understood why. Her entire life was ahead of her.

Chapter 7

WELCOME TO VIETNAM

"We have been too often disappointed by the optimism of the American leaders, both in Vietnam and Washington, to have faith any longer in the silver linings they find in the darkest clouds…we are mired in a stalemate that could only be ended by negotiation, not victory."

— WALTER CRONKITE,

CBS News anchor, February 27, 1968

"If I've lost Cronkite, I've lost middle America."

PRESIDENT LYNDON JOHNSON,

looking up from the TV, to his aides, February 27, 1968

"As you begin your service in Vietnam, you are joining with military personnel and civilian technicians from nations in a Free World team dedicated to assisting the people of South Vietnam to resist aggression…Your tour in Vietnam will be a challenge, but, as in the case of all genuine challenges, its accomplishment will give you the real satisfaction of a job well done."

—COMMANDER CREIGHTON ABRAM,

Stars and Stripes, Summer-Fall, 1968

Many American soldiers who were drafted into the military during the Vietnam War came from lower income families, the poor and the working class. They came from rural areas like those in northern Maine, from the towns and farming communities across the nation. I'd read that only 20 percent were actually from middle class families, and that very few belonged to the upper class. Because local and state draft boards operated under a "quota system," they were each required to choose a certain number of men to be drafted. It was common knowledge that some draft boards could occasionally be tampered with, showing favoritism and therefore deferments to certain young men from well-connected families, or within their own personal relationships.

Ray shortly after arriving in Vietnam. Notice the smile.

The draft, or conscription, wasn't a new concept. Compulsory enrollment for service in a country's armed forces has existed since 2700 BC, during what is known as the "Age of the Pyramid Builders." But I had enlisted once I was drafted, so it was time to spend my year in Vietnam and get it over with. Going into that war zone might have been easier if I knew what my job there would be. Yet no one I asked had ever heard of WDMET. I must have read that cryptic language on my orders a hundred times: *for fur asg to USA WDMET.* For further assignment to USA WDMET.

We were two days being processed at Oakland Army Base in the San Francisco Bay Area. We went through a ton of paperwork and then were given our combat fatigues and our shots, twenty-eight in all. As though we were kids getting ready for school, we followed orders to wear our khaki trousers and short-sleeved khaki shirts. Given the climate we were headed to, it made sense. A couple of days later we were put aboard a bus for nearby Travis Air Force Base where we boarded a Continental Airlines flight. As the plane gained altitude, San Francisco twinkled below us in a thousand lights.

It was a 26-hour flight to Bien Hoa, just northeast of Saigon. You gotta hand it to the military. It was a great send-off, an air-conditioned Boeing 707 with pretty stewardesses waiting on us. There was a ripple of nervous excitement throughout the cabin. Some guys slept. Others talked about where they'd be stationed and what their MOS was. Still others, like me, didn't feel up to conversation. The stewardesses went out of their way to make us comfortable. They came by often to ask if we needed a blanket, a pillow, a magazine, a soft drink. It was as if they wanted to protect us. Rookie soldiers going to Vietnam were called *newbies*. We were almost *all* newbies on that plane. Those stewardesses must have looked at each of our faces and wondered which ones wouldn't make the return flight. It wasn't a good year to be headed to Vietnam. But there I was.

Volumes could be written on *just one year* in the complicated history of Vietnam. When we American boys were growing up around the country, riding our bikes around our hometowns, going to a drive-in movie, and hoping to kiss a girl for the first time, how could we know that threads were being woven half-way around the globe in a bloody tapestry that would affect us the rest of our lives. And that's if we were lucky enough to live. But if I looked at the war through my own personal ladder of events, the summary would go something like this.

In 1941, a year before my father married my mother and left for his own stint in the U.S. Army, a key figure in the story, Nguyen Sinh Cung, returned to his birth country of Vietnam after thirty years of traveling the world in self-imposed exile. His name was Nguyen

Sinh Cung, but he had just begun calling himself Ho Chi Minh, a combination of Vietnamese names that means "He who has been enlightened." He soon formed a national coalition called the *Viet Minh* to lead the independence movement to free his homeland from the Japanese occupation. He had been raised by a well-educated father who refused, in protest, to learn or speak French when Vietnam was still under French rule.

In 1946, the year I was born, we had just witnessed the end of World War II. The Japanese had surrendered a few months earlier, just days after the United States dropped the world's first deployed atomic bomb on Hiroshima, and then Nagasaki, immediately killing over 100,000 people. With Japan's surrender, the government of France declared it would restore French control in Indochina. Ho Chi Minh stood before a massive crowd in Hanoi and declared, "Vietnam has the right to be a free and independent country." In December of that same year came the outbreak of the First Indochina War as French colonial forces battled to control Vietnam.

In the spring of 1950, a year before I started kindergarten and the superintendent of schools visited my parents to warn them against speaking French at home, President Harry Truman offered military assistance to non-Communist forces in Indochina. The United States sent aid, and the French did the training. Thus began our country's involvement in Vietnam.

In 1954, when my father had his first heart attack, a battle that lasted 55 days was fought between the French and Vietnamese forces, with thousands of casualties on both sides. This was the Battle of Dien Bien Phu. Many historians believe that it was a defining moment in what was to come in Southeast Asia. President Eisenhower refused to involve American troops. "I cannot conceive of a greater tragedy for America than to get heavily involved now in an all-out war in any of those regions." Two months later, his administration had a change of heart and military aid was sent to the French.

That summer, the Geneva Accords were signed. With the crumbling of the French empire and France's painful withdrawal, the country of Vietnam split into north and south. Ngo Dinh Diem, who had just returned to the region from France, was put in temporary control of what would soon become South Vietnam, although neither the U.S. nor the French were convinced of his ability to unite his people. But they had no better substitute for president.

Ho Chi Minh and his Viet Minh forces were allowed to regroup in the north, and the Democratic Republic of Vietnam became a one-party government located in Hanoi. The Geneva agreement allowed that for a period of 300 days the populace could move back and forth between the north and the south. With the help of the American CIA, a campaign was begun by Diem to encourage inhabitants, especially Vietnamese Catholics, to move to his part of the country. The campaign slogan was "God Has Gone South."

The slogan was a success since nearly a million people followed its advice. They were mostly Catholics and would become a future power base for Diem. The CIA warned him to downplay religion, given the anti-Catholic bias in American politics. In fact, the majority of Vietnamese were Buddhists. However, a major flaw in the agreement to allow freedom of movement for 300 days was that as the French departed, thousands of covert *Viet Minh* infiltrated cities, towns, and villages in the south. The repercussions of these decisions would be felt for many years to come, not just in Southeast Asia, but in the lives of Americans who were still children at the time.

In 1955, when I was collecting pop bottles, mowing lawns, and shoveling the snow, the last French forces finally left Indochina, and the first U.S. military advisors arrived in South Vietnam to help build Diem's army. President Eisenhower offered military and financial assistance to the new nation. And the Pentagon began directly supplying military aid to Saigon.

In 1956, when Ginger and I were delivering the *Bangor Daily News* on those safe and quiet streets in northern Maine, a new word was coined across the globe, *Viet Cong.* The government-controlled press in Saigon first printed it as an abbreviated version of *Viet Nam Cong-San,* or "Vietnamese communist."

In 1961, as I was having the last photograph taken with my father, the newly elected president, John Fitzgerald Kennedy, vowed in his inaugural address to continue President Eisenhower's policy of support for Diem's government in South Vietnam. He reiterated Eisenhower's belief that if one country toppled to communism, the one next to it would also topple, in what would become known to Americans as the "Domino Theory."

In August of that same year, the month my father died, the president of South Vietnam asked President Kennedy to conduct herbicidal warfare in his country against the enemy in North Vietnam. After a debate in Washington as to the ethics of this action, it was finally pointed out that the British had already set a legal precedent for herbicides and defoliants during the Malayan Emergence, their own guerilla-style jungle warfare which had dragged on for a dozen years, ending in 1960. And, after all, folks in America were using these weed killers in their vegetable gardens.

President Kennedy authorized the military to spray the rivers, rice paddies, farmlands, and jungles along the Ho Chi Minh Trail. This was intended to deprive the Viet Cong of food sources, and defoliate that hideaway tunnel through the jungle which the enemy used to transport people and weapons to South Vietnam. Because the 55-gallon drums they were stored in had colored stripes wrapped around their middles, these "tactical-use" chemicals—Agent Blue, Agent Green, Agent Purple, Agent Pink, Agent White, and Agent Orange—were given the poetic name "Rainbow Herbicides." The military first started spraying the terrain in Vietnam with Agent Blue.

In 1963, the year I was working part-time at Zayre's, memorizing the information on electric carving knives and having milk with my pizza after work, there were 16,000 American military advisers in Vietnam. But the war was still being waged mostly from Washington,

D.C. In a news broadcast from early November, it was reported that Ngo Dinh Diem, the President of South Vietnam, and his younger brother, who acted as his top advisor, were captured in a coup by the Army of the Republic of Vietnam and brutally murdered. I likely missed this news since I was doing my best to survive the lingerie department at Zayre's. That the CIA was involved in this coup was much to President Kennedy's disapproval. A series of generals would take Diem's place for the following few years of unsettled leadership in the country. Three weeks after the deaths, our own country was thrown into a state of mourning when President Kennedy was assassinated in Dallas.

In 1964, a few months after sister Del had her first baby and Grammie Gagnon/Lebel passed away, an incident took place off the coast of North Vietnam and southern China in the Gulf of Tonkin. According to our military's version, three torpedo boats belonging to the North Vietnamese Navy pursued the *USS Maddox*, a destroyer that was in the gulf gathering intelligence. When the *Maddox* fired three warning shots, it was attacked with machine gun fire and torpedoes. In the battle that followed, the *Maddox* fired 280 shells at the North Vietnamese boats, and sustained a single bullet hole herself. No American lives were lost. The enemy lost four sailors with another six wounded. It was reported that a similar battle occurred two days later. But it was soon revealed that this battle was nothing more than false radar images, now known as "Tonkin ghosts."

Within a week, and in response to this incident, the United States Congress passed a joint resolution known as the Gulf of Tonkin Resolution. It gave President Lyndon Johnson authorization to do what was deemed necessary to block the spread of communism in Southeast Asia. And it could be done without a formal declaration of war by Congress. The senate approved the resolution 88 votes to two. Of the two senators who opposed, Senator Gruening, a Democrat from Alaska, stated that we would be, "sending our American boys into combat in a war in which we have no business, which is not our war, into which we have been misguidedly drawn, which is steadily being escalated." The second "nay" vote was cast by Senator Morse, a Democrat from Oregon, who believed "this resolution to be a historic mistake." Critics of the war saw this overwhelming majority as having given the Johnson administration "a blank check" in Vietnam.

In 1965, as I was preparing to graduate from Presque Isle High School, one of the generals who led the coup against President Diem that resulted in his murder became the country's new president. His name is the one that Americans would know best and longest, Nguyen Van Thieu. A month after President Johnson told his national security advisers, "I've had enough of this," over a hundred American fighter-bombers began attacks on targets in North Vietnam as a part of Operation Rolling Thunder. The engagement was expected to last eight weeks, but would endure for three years.

A week after the bombing began, the first American combat troops arrived in Vietnam when 3500 Marines landed at China Beach to defend the nearby air base at Da Nang. President Johnson also authorized the use of napalm, a petroleum-based jelly used in incendiary bombs that would explode on impact with a downpour of pellets. In a Gallup Poll, when asked if they thought the USA made a mistake in sending troops to Vietnam, 61 percent of Americans polled said "No." In December's issue of *Reader's Digest* magazine, Richard Nixon, the former Vice-President under Eisenhower, wrote an article stating, "There can be no substitute for victory when the objective is the defeat of communist aggression." By the end of 1965, approximately 184,313 American soldiers were on site in South Vietnam, compared to 23,310 a year earlier.

In 1966, when I signed up for Biblical History at St. Thomas University in Fredericton, the dioxin of choice to defoliate the jungles in Vietnam and destroy enemy crops was Agent Orange, which had beat out all of the other "Rainbow Herbicides." Shortly after I flunked Biblical History, American prisoners of war were marched through the streets of Hanoi and attacked by an angry mob. In protest of Diem's pro-Catholic policies, and his discrimination against the majority Buddhist population, Buddhist monks and activists took to the streets in South Vietnam.

In October, when I finished counting aphids on potato plants and rode the bus to Bangor for induction into the military, the number of American soldiers in South Vietnam was 385,300, not counting the 60,000 sailors stationed offshore. The South Vietnamese, our allied troops, numbered 735,900. In all, 6,000 American men died that year and another 30,000 were wounded.

In 1967, when I was being trained in X-ray technology and as a combat medic at Fort Sam Houston, 485,600 American troops were on the ground in South Vietnam. And that strange word *Viet Cong* was so familiar to American soldiers, and the American public, that it was often used in conversation around dinner tables after Walter Cronkite brought us the evening news.

By 1968, as I was boarding an air-conditioned Boeing 707 headed for Vietnam, and being pampered by the stewardesses, there were 536,100 American troops there ahead of me. The first Tet Offensive had riddled the country with fighting a few months earlier, in January. And Tet II had just finished. A few weeks earlier, on the last day of March at 9:30 pm Eastern time, President Johnson had shocked the country and most of his top aides when, in his speech to the nation, he said these words: "I shall not seek, and I will not accept, the nomination of my party for another term as your president." The Vietnam War would soon belong to Richard Nixon.

The hundreds of thousands of people who were lost in Vietnam on both sides took many years and a lot of warfare to realize. And, as in the backdrop of any war in history were the Shakespearean characters, those politicians and generals who made the decisions that carried the fighting forward. In the aftermath, after the bombs stopped falling, after the explosions ceased and the smoke finally cleared, lying in the wreckage and between the pages of history would be the bodies of millions of innocent lives.

As the plane flew through the night sky, with miles of dark ocean rolling beneath us, I thought of Shirley and our last meeting. It hurt me deeply that she had seemed so nonchalant about saying goodbye. She was my last connection to the old days, to northern Maine and our roots there. She had changed my life in more ways than one. In the past year I had given a lot of thought to staying in the military. I had grown to like the comfort of boundaries and limitations. The military would always need X-ray techs and I was moving up quickly in rank. But I had held back on thoughts of making the army my career and it was mostly because of Shirley. I knew from our talks that she wanted a nursing career that was on stable ground, not one where she had to pack up and move every time the wind blew a new assignment my way. With our breakup, when my time was up, I could reenlist if I wanted to. That was, if I survived a year in Vietnam.

Twenty-six hours later, and after refueling at Andersen Air Force Base on Guam, we landed at Bien Hoa in the middle of the night. This was a mutual operating base for both the U.S. Air Force and the Vietnam Armed Forces. Bien Hoa was so accustomed to a rocket or mortar hit that it had been nicknamed "Rocket Alley." When the plane landed, firefights were going on along the perimeter, with an occasional incoming rocket. "Keep your heads down," was the only advice we were given. The plane didn't even taxi up to a gate or a building that we could get into fast. It came to a stop in the middle of the runway. I suspect those non-military pilots wanted to get out of there as fast as they could.

The next thing I knew the doors opened to oppressive heat and a couple hundred soldiers said good-bye to air conditioning as we scrambled down the steps. We were put on buses and taken a few miles down the road to Long Binh, the largest U.S. Army base in Vietnam, with over 50,000 personnel. Long Binh was a major supply facility that the U.S. Army had built just outside Bien Hoa, about 20 miles northeast of the capital of Saigon. It was used as a logistics center and major command headquarters by the army, and had been attacked during the earlier Tet Offensive. I had no idea how long I'd be there until they sent me down to Tan Son Nhut, near Saigon.

Within a few days of being *in country*, as soldiers called it, I started trying to familiarize myself with that part of the world that would be my home for the next year. Lying completely within the tropics, Vietnam is a long and narrow country, running a thousand miles from north to south, and a little smaller than California in acreage. It's an ancient country steeped in traditions and histories that we Americans couldn't even imagine. The first thing that struck me as different was the smell, putrid, as if something was continually in the process of decay and mixed with diesel fuel. We had been put in barracks that were really partitioned walls with canvas roofs. But what I saw of the out-lying villages during my time in Long Binh made those barracks look fancy. The roads were all dirt, with dust flying up under the wheels of passing trucks and jeeps, or carts pulled by water buffalo. Villagers were living in what Americans would call shacks, many of them fabricated from tin cans. Naked children played in the dirt.

On Highway 1, the road leading past the base and going north to Da Nang, or south to Saigon, was a settlement of shacks known as Widow's Village. It was home to the widows and orphans of killed ARVN soldiers, our allies. The government paid them small pensions and the American troops at Long Binh often hired the women to fill sand bags or do laundry and other chores. During the Tet Offensive earlier that year, the village had been slowly infiltrated by Viet Cong who took over the shacks. They then began rocket and mortar attacks on Long Binh, which brought our forces into the fray.

When the Battle of Widow's Village was over, fifty Viet Cong lay dead.

The streets after monsoon rains

The month of May in Vietnam meant mostly hot weather. The rains didn't start until June. For nearly two weeks in the sweltering heat, which was broken by an occasional steamy rainfall in the afternoons, I cleaned latrines at Long Binh. When you're dealing with that many soldiers, you need latrines more than a good jail. It was a nasty job that smelled even worse than it looked. But at least it got my mind off Shirley for a time. As I waited to be sent down to Saigon, we pulled steel drums up out of the ground beneath wooden toilets and set the waste on fire with diesel fuel. Early one morning, a 122-millimeter rocket took out one of the latrines. I was almost sorry it hadn't taken them *all* out. That was my first introduction to Chinese-made missiles that didn't care *where* they landed, so long as they landed and did some damage.

If any of us rookies had wondered what the sounds and smells of war would be like, we were learning fast. Much to my surprise and even anger, I was given nighttime guard duty along the base perimeter. I soon learned that we were expected to do whatever needed doing, regardless of our assigned jobs. If no combat soldiers were around, a company clerk might be handed an M-16. There were several incursions with the enemy during my time at Long Binh, including a fire fight when North Vietnamese infiltrators broke into the perimeter.

Welcome to Saigon! Photo by John Stephenson.

On June 6th, I finally got my orders to report to Tan Son Nhut Air Base, on the southeast outskirts of Saigon. The next afternoon I was put aboard a helicopter and flown down to Tan Son Nhut, which took only a few minutes. It was a relief to leave the smelly latrines behind. A jeep was waiting for me at the helipad when I arrived, driven by the company clerk. I assumed he'd take me to headquarters where I would finally receive my job description.

"I'll drive you into Saigon," the clerk said. "To your billet."

"Saigon?" I asked. "Why not the barracks with the other guys?" But at least I could check combat medic off my list of concerns. Combat medics weren't put in billets, but sent to where the fighting was.

The clerk hunched his shoulders.

"Tomorrow you'll meet Colonel Ostrom, our unit commander. He'll explain everything."

Now I started getting really paranoid. This wasn't typical of the military. If I were going to be assigned to a medical unit surely it was time to inform me. We hopped in his jeep and he drove me from the base into Saigon, about three miles away. The next thing I knew, I was speeding through Saigon in a military jeep. The city smelled of the sidewalk garbage that had lain for days in the tropical sun, waiting for disposal. That rotting smell was mixed with the exhaust from too many vehicles that clogged the streets. Many of the cars were American and over twenty years old. Here and there were the bombed ruins of what had been shops and buildings. Civilians were digging amidst the rubble. The noise in Saigon was continual and deafening, with military trucks and jeeps intermingling with motorbikes and cycling rickshaws called pedicabs.

There was no logic to the flow of traffic, with vehicles constantly cutting in front of each other. Amid the honking cars and motorbikes, local farmers were pulling wooden carts. Live animals such as cackling chickens and grunting pigs were also carted to the marketplace for sale, along with dragon fruits, papayas, mangos, and spices. Colorful shop signs advertising foods and services seemed to be everywhere. The women wore long blouses with slits in the sides, over what looked like pajama bottoms. On their heads were pointed hats, and some carried umbrellas for shade from the hot sun. Their baskets were filled with vegetables like cabbages, spinach, and bamboo shoots. Most of the food was new to me, plants I'd never seen before. Along with tubs of strange-looking fish, plucked birds, and hanging sausages were the carcasses of animals I didn't recognize.

"This is Binh Tay Market," said the clerk, when he noticed the surprise on my face. "We're in Cholon, the largest Chinatown in the world. This part of the city caught hell in the recent fighting. It's amazing how fast the locals bounce back."

I could only stare. Beeping horns and the racket of street vendors blended with dozens of children begging a passing GI for whatever was in his pockets. Vietnamese policemen walked among the crowd, noticeable by their white gloves and white belts. Here and there a Buddhist temple appeared, with magnificent architecture that was also new to me. Cholon was a noisy canvas of bright colors and foreign sounds, an alien world from the quiet one I had known back in Maine. Beyond the stench and the racket was the knowledge that danger could be waiting. Communist sympathizers lurked on every street corner. The second phase of Tet had just died down, but there was always a flare-up somewhere with a 122-millimeter rocket occasionally hitting wherever it happened to land.

The clerk pulled the jeep over to the edge of a street and braked. We sat there idling.

"See this street?" he asked. I nodded, but it looked just like any other street in Saigon. "This street is where the photo was taken. You know, the one where the general executed that VC prisoner? See that white building? That's in the photo."

I knew then what he was referring to. A photograph taken a few months earlier had swept around the world to become a visual symbol of the war's brutality. A Viet Cong prisoner, his eyes squinted and his face grimacing, was a second away from a bullet exploding into his brain, fired by a South Vietnamese general and national police chief, a man who was our ally. What the picture didn't say was that the VC prisoner was our enemy. He was in Saigon during the first Tet offensive to kill Americans and their allies, which he had already done with no hesitation. He had just slit the throats of a South Vietnamese colonel, his wife, six children, and his 80-year-old mother.

War has no easy blacks and whites, no simple markers. Most days, war is all gray. No matter how you looked at it, it's hell on both sides. I didn't know how I was going to last a year in that place. But one thought kept going through my mind: *Focus. You're a long-timer now, with a year to go. Count the days, one at a time. Mark them off carefully until you're finally a short-timer. And then run, don't walk, to board that plane back to the States.*

Exterior view of Ray's billet in Saigon

After careening down a few more streets, we arrived at an old four-story hotel in the heart of Cholon. I followed him up the steps and waited until he unlocked the door. My billet was a single room, small and sparsely furnished. There was a wooden desk against one wall with a chair next to it. A hot plate sat on top of the desk. In one corner was a narrow cot with some bedding. There was nothing on the walls.

"Your team isn't assigned to a mess hall," the clerk said. "You'll be given extra money to buy food at the Post Exchange. We call it the **PX**. You can cook here or eat out."

"We don't eat at the mess hall?"

He shook his head, but offered no explanation.

"Get yourself a good *mamma-san*," he said. "One that doesn't have any kids." I knew what a *mamma-san* was from back at Long Binh and Widow's Village.

They were house keepers, girls and adult women who would make beds, sweep floors, do laundry, sew buttons on a shirt, polish shoes, anything a soldier needed done. It didn't cost much and yet it was good money for their family. When they worked, those who had no choice often brought their children.

"I don't mind the kids," I said. He didn't seem to be listening. He had a memorized list of items in his head to tell me. He'd probably given the same speech to new soldiers a hundred times or more.

"There are steel drums on the roof where you can take a shower." He pointed up, as if maybe I wouldn't know how to find the roof. "Get your *mamma-san* to fill the drums with water each day. The sunlight will heat it."

The billet was primitive all right, but it was a couple of rungs up from a bunk in a typical barracks. It was certainly private. Were X-ray technicians this valuable to the military in Vietnam?

"Where are my team members?" I asked.

"Some are here," he said. "Some are in other billets around the city."

What the hell? I thought. Why had they put us in separate living quarters, as if to isolate us? Saigon was off-base, hardly a safe place to put an American soldier. In addition to the Viet Cong sympathizers, rockets were still exploding all over the city. At least the base was a somewhat protected area.

When he closed the door and left, I threw my duffel bag onto the cot and stood staring at the bare walls. I realized I was hungry. I could probably find something to eat at one of the little cafes I'd seen along the street, so long as I could recognize what the hell I was eating. Some of those carcasses looked like rats and snakes. The next day I'd buy some groceries. I knew all about hot plates having cooked my food on one while I was holed up at Martin Manor in Presque Isle. Martin Manor now loomed like a castle in my mind. I looked at my watch. It was 6 pm in Vietnam. In New England, the sun would just be rising and Shirley would be getting up for the day, twelve time zones away. She would be excited about the upcoming engagement party for her friend. But a lot more than time zones was separating us now.

The clerk opened the door to my room without knocking.

"Shit, I forgot to tell you," he said. "Bobby Kennedy just died."

Chapter 8

THE ELITE TEAM

"The uniqueness of the Vietnam War places great emphasis on employing experts in a number of fields. One such group of highly specialized military personnel is the US Army's Wound Data Munitions Effectiveness Team. The 45-member team is composed of experts from both combat arms and medical corps. Studies based on the findings of this unique group of men could possibly change the current ideas in military weaponry as well as improve the treatment of US causalities in great measure."

—PEOPLE IN THE NEWS,
The Stars & Stripes military magazine, 1967.

It was a long and restless night. Sometimes I'd hear an explosion that brought me wide awake. I tried not to think of one of those damn rockets headed for that cheesy hotel. I tossed and turned until dawn finally came. I found the steel drums on the roof, an army green with wide orange stripes around them. I showered with cool water since the sun hadn't time to heat it. Then I dressed and walked down the street, hoping to find a place that sold coffee. The marketplace was already alive with its usual racket. Along with the smell of that garbage was the fresher aromas of cooking food as vendors sautéed dishes on the sidewalk. I didn't see any bacon and eggs. Unless I found a restaurant that served American food, I'd be cooking meals in my billet. I bought a cup of coffee at a small café, but it tasted like shit. I'd pick up some groceries later. The company clerk had pointed out a huge **PX** and commissary in Cholon where I could shop.

I got back to the hotel a few minutes before 8 o'clock and stood waiting outside. In no time a jeep pulled up, the clerk behind the wheel. I opened the passenger door and got in. We wove our way out of the crazy traffic in Cholon, through the morning throng of people, and headed the short distance to Tan Son Nhut. To reach the main gate to the base we circled the Tomb of Pigneau de Behaine, in round-about fashion.

I would learn that Pierre Pigneau was a French missionary who had come from France in the mid-1700s to convert the people to Catholicism. He was instrumental in helping to establish the Nguyen Dynasty. When Pigneau died in 1799, a mausoleum was built by the emperor he had befriended, in a tiny village called Tan Son Nhut. A couple of decades later, a new emperor resisted Catholicism in his Buddhist country. He banned foreign priests after killing a few. The French were riled up enough back in France to defend their priests and launch an intervention in that part of the world. It was the beginning of French involvement in Indochina. Civilization slowly grew up around Pigneau's tomb that had once rested in pastoral countryside. Now, it sat near the main entrance to a busy American military base.

The clerk dropped me off at the mortuary to await further instructions.

I noticed two soldiers working at tables set up outside the trailers. The tables sat atop a concrete pad and had a canvas roof over them to protect the workers from the sun. I walked over for a closer look. I was shocked to see that the tables were littered with human bones. The men were examining each one and then placing them in anatomical order. On the second table lay an almost complete skeleton.

"Is this what I think it is?" I asked the soldier nearest me. He nodded. "We're hoping to get these guys identified and sent home."

These were bones that had been found in areas of combat. Some had lain in rice paddies, or within the steamy jungle, or were exposed to the hot sun. Bodies could become mummified and turn skeletal in a matter of weeks in that tropical climate. Exposure to insects, animals, and the air didn't help either. It was discomforting to know that these had been real soldiers. This wasn't a biology class or a television show. Those bones had once been flesh-and-blood boys or men from Ohio, or Utah, or even my home state of Maine. These trained personnel had the job of reassembling the bones to find out who they had once belonged to. It was like putting back together a picture that had been ripped to shreds by war.

"We rely on what information we're given," the second soldier said. "Where these bones were found is important. You know, if any soldiers are missing near a certain place of combat. If we have dental charts, we use them. We take height into consideration. This guy here, as you can see, was about six feet tall."

"Sometimes there are personal effects found nearby," the first soldier added. "Dog tags. Jewelry. Once we can identify the soldier, we send the bones over to the mortuary and they ship them home."

A jeep pulled up in front of the trailers and a colonel got out. It was my commanding officer, Colonel Thomas Ostrom. I saluted him.

"I bet you've got a lot of questions for me, don't you, soldier?" he asked.

"Yes, sir."

"Follow me," the colonel said.

As we walked past the first trailer, I looked into the building that was the mortuary. Inside the open door I saw silver-colored boxes stacked high. They looked like shiny aluminum caskets. The colonel noticed my gaze.

Empty transfer cases

Empty Transfer cases used to carry remains of soldiers back home

"Transfer cases," he said. "Our casualties go back to the States in those. We're pretty cramped right now, especially with these recent enemy attacks. But we'll be moving into a bigger facility by September. Then all the units will be in a central location. Our personal effects depot is at Camp Redball, a couple miles north of here. That's where all personal belongings are stored before being shipped home to the next of kin."

We climbed the steps to one of the trailers and went inside, which was a lot like stepping into an oven. Without windows there was no breeze, even if there had been a breeze in that tropical climate. Two ceiling fans spun overhead, sending down waves of stale air. The generators outside kept up a steady buzz that I found hard to ignore. But at least this trailer had X-ray equipment set up over a table. I saw a radiation booth in the corner. These were the tools of my trade, and I felt a sense of relief at last. A sergeant, tall and lanky, stepped into the room. He was wearing sunglasses, which he took off. He gave me a welcoming smile.

"This is James Flowers," the colonel said. "He's our chief radiologist. Now let me answer some of those questions you have. WDMET stands for Wound Data Munitions Effectiveness Team." It sounded like he had said *wid-met.*

I heard the *thwap-thwap-thwap* of another incoming Huey to the helipad.

"I'll train you," said Flowers. "Don't worry. You're in good hands. I also happen to know a couple of pretty waitresses in Saigon."

I nodded. But I wasn't sure why wounded soldiers would be brought to that trailer for X-rays and not to the hospital.

"WDMET gets its orders directly from the Pentagon," Ostrom added, "and not MACV. We've been in country for a year now."

The Pentagon? MACV was the Military Assistance Command Vietnam. They were headquartered near the main gate at Tan Son Nhut in a huge, air-conditioned complex. The clerk had pointed it out to me as we drove past. MACV ran the show when it came to the entire military operation in Vietnam. Before I could ask about this, two soldiers came into the X-ray room carrying a human remains pouch by its straps.

They hoisted it up onto the examining table in front of us. Flowers gave me a cautious look, as if sizing up what I might do. One of the soldiers unzipped the bag from head to toe, and opened it. The other helped him lift up the body of a young soldier, probably 20 years old. He was what the military called a "grunt," a foot soldier or infantryman, the kind of soldier you learn to respect, admire, and pity, all at the same time. They were the soldiers who fought the enemy up close and personal, and suffered the most causalities in Vietnam. His face had a growth of beard, as grunts out in the field often did. But it was a bloody mess, dotted with shrapnel. His eyes were open. I had seen only a few dead people in my life, all family members and all properly prepared and lying in caskets.

"He stepped on a mine," one of the soldiers told Colonel Ostrom.

They slid the bag down under the body and pulled it off the end of the table. The grunt's left leg had been blown away from above the knee. Shattered bone was sticking out of that leg in splinters. There was a hole in his chest area and his intestines were protruding. One of the men reached inside the bag and lifted out a mangled leg, missing the foot, which he placed gently next to the body. They rolled up the body bag and left the room. I fought off a wave of nausea.

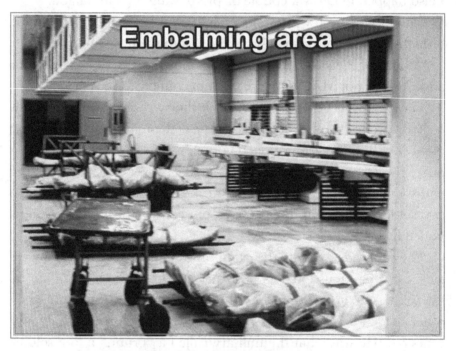

The embalming area at the morgue, showing some of the body bags. It was here that the remains were prepared for their flight home.

"We reuse the body bags," Ostrom said. "We have civilians who hose them down near the mortuary."

I stood frozen, staring at the table. Mixed in with the odor of formaldehyde, and the heat and humidity of Vietnam, was the rancid smell of decaying flesh and body gases. I had never smelled anything like it before, and I was soon to miss the latrines back at Long Binh. This wasn't the smell of a butchered animal or a bagged deer during hunting season. I felt the room spin around me.

"He's got a tourniquet on that leg," Sergeant Flowers said, and pointed. "Medics must have tried to save him."

"Gauvin, you're now part of an exclusive team," said Colonel Ostrom. "Handpicked. We study and evaluate combat casualties. WDMET is the largest research study in wartime history."

Did he say casualties?

Holy shit, I thought. *This must be a mistake. I'm not supposed to be doing this.*

I couldn't take my eyes off the dead soldier. He was so damn young. But hell, Vietnam was a war for the young. As someone once said, "Young men will go to war because they don't believe they'll die." But in reality, no young soldier wanted to die. They didn't want to fight anyone. They wanted to live, to fall into love or out of love. They wanted to have families and careers. They wanted to leave good memories behind when it came their time to die, at home, and not half-way around the globe. Lying before me was the son of some woman who would soon be grieving. He was someone's brother, someone's best friend. He was the lover of a young girl who was waiting in one of the fifty states for him to come home.

I thought back to how proud I'd been of my test scores during training. I had worked very hard to get those top scores. I had been *hand-picked?* This is where that hard work had gotten me? And then I felt a stinging wave of guilt. I was still alive.

"We can't help this unfortunate soldier," Colonel Ostrom was saying now. "But what we learn here at Tan Son Nhut can help save future lives. The wounds you'll be X-raying will tell us how to improve our helmets and flak jackets. In other words, how to protect our soldiers from enemy munitions."

Sweat was rolling off me now. It felt like I was being baked alive inside that trailer. Above the annoying drone of the generators, I could hear another incoming chopper. More dead soldiers for the mortuary. The putrid air filled my nostrils.

"There are thirty CPs around the country," Ostrom added. "Those are collecting points. Casualties are taken there from the battlefield by chopper or whatever works. We have WDMET personnel who go out in the field to the CPs and choose the bodies that have specific wounds for us to study. Those bodies come to us first and usually by truck."

"We X-ray and record the wounds," Flowers said. "In this case, did the shrapnel penetrate his liver or spleen? Maybe his lungs? Then the pathologists do a full autopsy, internal and external. When we're done, we send them over to the mortuary for embalming. The mortuary sends them home. You'll get the hang of it."

"Can you handle this, Gauvin?" Colonel Ostrom asked me.

They both looked at me, waiting for a reaction. My face must have shown how I felt, that everything I knew and expected of the world, of my life on the planet, had just been swept away. The thought that kept running through my head was, *Can I refuse this? Can I say no? And if I* do *have a choice, then why the hell don't they tell me?*

"Yes, Sir," I said. My head felt as if it would explode.

"If you need any advice," the colonel said, "come find me. Sergeant Flowers here will show you the ropes."

When Colonel Ostrom left, the sergeant looked at me.

"I'll tell you a little secret," he said. "MACV doesn't want us here. We'd be bad for the soldiers' morale if they found out about us. Shit, we're worse than the mortuary guys. I mean, who wants to end up being autopsied? When Westmoreland found out about the study, he made it known we weren't welcome in Vietnam. Most of us were pretty happy about that. But then some high-ranking civilian who headed up our initial team, a GS-18, went to D.C. and pulled some strings for Ostrom."

GS stood for *General Schedule* and was the pay scale used by the U.S. Civil Service, with the lowest rank receiving the GS-1 salary, all the way up to GM-15. The three levels above that were considered "super grades," so the guy was definitely a bigwig. And now I understood the secrecy. Not only would we be bad for morale, but what if families back in the States learned that autopsies were being performed on their fallen sons, fathers, and brothers in the name of research? There were already enough protests and anger over the war. Now it made perfect sense. That was why we were outside the perimeter of the base with our own noisy generators running non-stop. It was why they put us in billets in Saigon, despite the occasional mortars and gunfire. It wouldn't be good if we slept in the barracks with the other soldiers, or ate next to them at the mess hall. What if one of us screwed up and mentioned the study?

"The new facility will be a better set-up than this," Sergeant Flowers said. "We'll have better ventilation and space. The mortuary will have 20 tables and a bigger freezer."

He pointed at the soldier on the table.

"We need to take off his clothing," he said. "The mortuary guys will check his pockets later to be sure they missed nothing back at the CP. You know, something that might embarrass his family or tarnish his reputation. He might have photos of naked Vietnamese girls. They also get rid of any drugs they find. Now and then a soldier saves a human trophy, like a shriveled-up ear."

All I could think of was getting it over with, and getting the hell out of there. I'd drive my jeep back to Cholon as fast as I could. Then, after I pounded my head against the wall in that piece-of-shit billet, I'd go up to the roof and stand beneath one of those drums with the orange stripes. I'd let the warm water wash away the smell, and I hoped that would be possible.

I forced myself to touch the first button. I took a deep breath, but breathing just brought the smell deeper into my lungs. A mixture of dried blood, formaldehyde, and death. It made me cough.

"You'll learn to breathe a new way," said Flowers. "It helps mask the smell. We need to X-ray that chest wound first."

He pushed the X-ray box that rode on ball bearings above the table. It rolled forward. I couldn't speak. I couldn't ask any questions. I had already started to move outside my body, rise above it so I could watch the action, unattached. I decided then and there to never mention what my new job in the military was when I wrote a letter home.

And if I was lucky enough to get back there one day, I would never speak of it to anyone. I had to believe this work would save lives in the future. I had no choice.

"I'm sorry to tell you this," Flowers said, "but this is a damn good day. It's gonna get a lot worse than this. Some bodies have been in delta water a couple weeks. Bloated. We call them Jolly Green Giants, or Floaters. Pilots burned in crashes? Rice Crispies. It sounds harsh, but it's not meant as disrespect. A sense of humor helps us do the job.

Sometimes, you'll have to fill wounds with chloroform to wash out the maggots before you can X-ray. Be careful, because your hands will often go right into the body tissue. You'll get used to it after a while. At least we're not over in the mortuary. When the body count goes up and Chinooks bring them in, instead of the smaller Hueys, they're piled high over there."

Sergeant Flowers glanced at me. I'm not sure if he saw dread or total shock on the newbie's face. He read the name on my shirt.

"Where are you from, Gauvin?" he asked.

I answered and then I put my hands onto the X-ray box and helped him position it over the soldier's chest.

There are three pictures of me that best document my experiences in Uncle Sam's army. In the first one, I'm twenty-one years old. I've just graduated from X-ray school at Fort Sam Houston as a technician. I'm wearing my lab coat and staring off to the left, arms linked behind my back, my face showing the pride I felt at that moment. I had graduated with top scores.

The second is of me in my uniform fatigues, newly arrived at Long Binh, one hand nonchalantly resting on my hip and a pleasant smile on my face. You wouldn't know by my eyes that I'd been cleaning latrines in the heat. There is nothing but confidence on my face.

The third photo was taken less than two months after I stepped into that trailer in early June so that Colonel Ostrom could enlighten me. "Gauvin, you're now part of an exclusive team. Hand-picked." In that last photo is the face of a young man who has already disappeared. It's a face frozen in melancholy, sorrow, and stress. The glimmer that was still in my eyes at Long Binh is already gone.

But I *did* learn to breathe a new way, holding my breath for seconds as I worked and then expelling it. I did learn to use humor to protect myself from the reality, a kind of fraternal humor I would recognize later on the popular television series *M.A.S.H.* I also learned that sometimes it was easier to talk to the soldier who was lying on my table. *This won't take long, buddy. You're helping out your fellow soldiers. Then you're going home.*

"Doc" Lane, Ray's unit commander at WDMET

Shortly after arriving at Tan Son Nhut, I was promoted to E-5. I also met Major Lane, the chief pathologist who would soon become a mentor to me. Major Lane had just returned from a month up at Da Nang, the smaller mortuary in the north where the Navy and Marines were also conducting a WDMET study. We were the Army, down in the south near Saigon, so most of us had no idea similar studies were going on up north. On the Tan Son Nhut lab team, there were about 15 of us over the course of the two years that the study was conducted.

Our field teams, the guys who selected the bodies with specific wounds and brought them to us, were mostly infantrymen who also did research with wounded soldiers, asking them questions such as "Why weren't you wearing your helmet?" The answer was easy. Those steel pot helmets worn in Vietnam were heavy, and they were hot as hell. Those field teams had a tough job, too. With a war still raging around them, their work was not as reliable as in a controlled environment such as we had. And it was dangerous to say the least.

There was a lot to learn that was new to me. The main weapons of war can be separated into *explosive munitions* such as artillery, grenades, rockets, mortars, bombs, mines, and improvised explosive devices. And *small arms* such as machine guns, rifles, and pistols. These were the munitions that had caused the wounds we were studying, and thus the "M" in WDMET. We were concerned with certain questions, such as whether weapon velocity was the most important factor in causing tissue damage. *No, it wasn't.* Was the exit wound always larger than an entrance wound? *No, it wasn't.* Was it correct that full metal-jacketed bullets would not fragment except in rare cases? *Bullets from the M-16 rifle will reliably fragment.* In a few months, I was made chief of the radiology department.

The task was gruesome, no other word for it. It was haunting and emotionally debilitating. But I found a certain solace in knowing that I was turning out reliable X-rays that were of the highest quality. What's more, with Major Lane's approval, I began to experiment. He was always quick to praise my work. Within a few weeks, I had invented a new X-ray technique for soft-tissue, often in multi-dimensional layers.

Colonel Ostrom came by occasionally, and when he did, he also commended me. Despite my surroundings, and despite my "patients," I felt a pride I thought I'd lost when Ostrom told me one day, "Thanks to the job you're doing, Gauvin, this is the very first time that exceptional quality X-rays are being done in the war theater." He pointed out that missiles inside the body that had been impossible to find previously could now be located with minimal difficulty.

I was determined to persevere, no matter what. But the bodies just kept coming. I knew the guys over in the mortuary were curious as to what we were doing, but they pretty much ignored us. Most times, with Saigon often under attack, we were just trying to get the job done and cover our asses. One day in particular, when pathology finished with an autopsy, I wheeled the body over to the mortuary. One of the guys there looked at it and asked, "Why him? He's got a bullet hole between his eyes. Surely you guys know what killed him?" Of course, those were the wounds we were studying to learn how to improve helmets. Or if a body was all in pieces, we might get a strange look from whoever at the mortuary took the gurney. I knew they were thinking that this poor soldier had stepped on a live mine. Why an autopsy? We were looking for shrapnel in the body, to see if any of the organs had been penetrated.

The new mortuary buildings that were opened in September, 1968.

I was not unhappy when we moved into the much larger, newly-built facility that September. It had an eight-foot-high fence around it made of thick plywood to keep us even more private. At the old mortuary, which had a fence half that height, an occasional soldier with a morbid curiosity about death, would try to see into the building. The new fence made that impossible. I was not unhappy, but I felt guilty. It was a better working environment for all of us, but it also meant that more American soldiers were dying in Vietnam.

In 1967, with 11,363 soldiers dead, the number was almost double 1966, which had recorded *triple* the number of deaths in 1965. It didn't take a genius to recognize the increase in numbers, so much so that the Army had the plans in motion to build the larger morgue. They were visionaries all right. In 1968, the number had risen to 16,899 American deaths, which meant that 70 percent of those soldiers came through the mortuary at Tan Son Nhut before going home for burial. The sound of Hueys and Chinooks landing at the helipad seemed constant. For those high-casualty battles, trucks rumbled in and C-130s landed on the tarmac. A bigger morgue was a gruesome military necessity.

Because the contractors who built the facility didn't know about WDMET—or perhaps they thought we'd be gone in a year and forgotten—the building was not radiation safe. Only our team wore radiation badges, which were evaluated each month to determine how much radiation we were receiving.

The more secretive we remained, the better. Morale among the soldiers at that point in the war was pretty low as it was. A lot of the soldiers in Vietnam were growing their hair long. Some had beards. Many were doing drugs and disrespecting their officers. You couldn't blame them. The body count was climbing by the day with no sign of letting up. The *couleur du jour* of the U.S. Army is a depressing drab olive. It was everywhere. But seeing those green body bags coming into my tiny lab was enough to cause my stomach muscles to immediately tighten. I figured an ulcer would be in my future, maybe more than one. I had no idea what wounds the body inside might have sustained, or if the soldier would be in several pieces afloat in body gases and fluids. Only unzipping the bag would bring an answer.

My hands also trembled at times as I wondered if I'd see a face I knew from back home, or basic training, or Fort Sam, or Fort Lewis, or Fort Belvoir. I knew the guys across the hall at the mortuary were seeing some of their friends in those bags. They were the ones who saw a river of dead bodies, after all. WDMET had our share, but they were casualties selected for our study. The mortuary guys got them all.

A few of our autopsies were done on soldiers who didn't die in combat, but by other means if Major Lane felt the wounds were interesting enough to study. One body that ended up in our lab was that of a young soldier killed by a tiger. I'm thankful that it was not during my watch that this body came in. I would learn fifty years later that he was a kid from Ohio, barely twenty years old, who had been in-country only six weeks. He and two other soldiers were on reconnaissance, searching for Viet Cong soldiers in isolated stretches of the jungle, one of the most dangerous jobs of the war.

Their first night out, they heard something following their Jeep and soon realized it was not human movement, but likely a tiger. They spent a sleepless night, sitting in the Jeep, their backs touching and each facing the jungle, his gun at the ready. The second night, the animal pounced in the dark, dragging the young soldier into the undergrowth. For two hours his buddies yelled his name, to no avail. When the helicopters arrived with the search mission, they found the body six hours later.

Major Lane felt the remains should be autopsied and studied. This was the first American casualty caused by a tiger attack and Lane and others felt it may not be the last. A couple more soldiers *were* attacked, one narrowly escaping death. The army, always reluctant to share news that might hold the military in a bad light, told this kid's family that he was missing in action. A week later, the story became that he had been alone on guard duty when he was attacked and killed by a tiger. Forty years would pass before one of the two soldiers who was spared that night called the PFC's sister in Mississippi to give her the full details of what had happened. As the animal's body flew over him in the dark, grabbing the PFC and dragging him off, the soldier had even tried to punch it.

*The original X-ray of the skull of the young soldier who was attacked
and killed by a tiger, 50 years later.*

I say I wasn't in the lab with Major Lane and that I didn't X-ray the body. But the truth is that there is no way of knowing. Was it so horrific that I blocked it out? Are the occasional flashbacks of seeing on my X-ray table a soldier I went to school with real, or did I imagine it? I was very aware that any soldiers I knew from Maine who were killed in our sector would be coming to TSN mortuary, and possibly to WDMET. I just can't be sure what happened during that year in hell.

As the days slowly passed, I fluctuated from despair over my job to expectation as I marked each day off the calendar. We stayed busy. When I wasn't doing X-rays, I often had other chores which might include cleaning up the godawful mess. Sometimes at the billet, when I fell exhausted into bed, I might find myself in northern Maine again. In one dream, it was snowing and I was still a boy. Huge white flakes were falling on Ginger and me as we walked from house to house delivering newspapers. One such night I woke smiling, something I rarely did anymore. I had dreamed of Ginger wagging his tail as he carried a newspaper in his mouth to give to a customer. I had taught him that trick, and my dog-loving clients always enjoyed it. They would pat his head as they took their paper. Then I heard the constant racket of Saigon outside my door and remembered where I really was.

With socializing so rare among our team members, and with me feeling a little safer in the billet than on the streets of Saigon, I did a lot of reading while lying on my narrow cot and drinking a beer or two from the PX. The military saw to it that we had

Outside the Tan Son Nhut gate

plenty of printed material. Every month, cargo planes landed on the runway at Tan Son Nhut with two million copies of American newspapers for the PX in Cholon. They also brought 150,000 magazines, which included everything from *Playboy* and *Mad,* to *Time* and *Newsweek,* to the *Harvard Business Review* and even *The American Journal of Psychiatry*. Also arriving monthly were 400,000 paperback books in every genre. But a newspaper I enjoyed for its simplicity and quick reading was *Stars and Stripes*, which arrived daily from Tokyo.

Stars and Stripes had an interesting history. In 1861, when Civil War soldiers from Illinois regiments set up camp in Bloomfield, Missouri, they noticed that the local newspaper office was empty. Deciding to print a slim paper that would record their activities, they called it the *Stars and Stripes*. By World War I, that same name was chosen but for a different newspaper, the one we still know today. Notable names who were once on the staff at *Stars and Stripes* from World War I onward to Vietnam were a mixture of seasoned newspapermen in uniform and young soldiers who might later seek a career in journalism or the arts. This group included Harold Ross, who came home from France to co-found *The New Yorker* magazine. Andy Rooney and Steve Kroft of *60 Minutes* fame were also on the staff, as was sportswriter Grantland Rice, Pulitzer Prize-winning cartoonist Bill Mauldin, and songwriter Shel Silverstein. It was the highest correspondence job in the army.

During the Vietnam War, the newspaper was printed daily in Tokyo, Japan. But it was written by a staff of five soldiers who were also photographers. They were holed up in a two-story villa in Saigon, but managed to spend four days a week out in the field talking to the troops. The Japanese plant where the paper was printed had a work force of thirty U.S. military, and about as many civilians on the staff. Any late-breaking news in Vietnam would be phoned to Tokyo by the writers in Saigon. Although authorized by the Department of Defense, the paper remained editorially independent under the First Amendment. Despite that freedom-of-speech umbrella, it was fairly watered-down and government-laundered.

Stars and Stripes had the usual military hand-outs about enemy numbers and various events in the combat zones. An article might be about the pink malaria pill that American soldiers hated taking daily since it could cause stomach upset and diarrhea.

There were comics and occasional illustrations to enlighten the newbies as to what the Viet Cong guerillas looked like. Some drawings showed grass and leaves glued to VC helmets, which they did for camouflage. For entertainment there might be snippets as to what the Beatles were up to, or what new films were in the theaters.

There was also a column called *Boondock Bards,* which printed poems written by in-country soldiers.

What I enjoyed most were the articles that educated us on Vietnamese history and social mores. They instructed our soldiers on how to intermingle with the Vietnamese civilians and treat them with respect. "The customs and traditions practiced by the people of the Republic of Vietnam, where you are a guest during your tour with the Free World Forces, may be traced back through many centuries." This was a lot of rhetoric, of course, since a *guest* is usually invited and doesn't tear up the place while visiting. And a *tour* should be to Niagara Falls. We were advised to leap headfirst into the Vietnamese culture. "The time to begin is now!" We were also reminded that our Yank ways might be misunderstood by our quiet and courteous "hosts."

If invited into a civilian home—the Vietnamese held their homes dear to their hearts—we were coached not to speak loudly or get too overly emotional. We were not to put our shoes on the furniture, or cross our legs so that our feet pointed toward a person or a shrine. Nor were we to force our opinions onto our hosts. We were not to shake hands first, or "be a back-slapper." American gestures were referred to as "booby traps" in one column I read. We were advised to save all our hand and arm signals for American use only. "The Vietnamese practice these rules of etiquette much more stringently than Americans, and violations of them are regarded seriously." It always struck me as ironic since we were pretty much shoving our opinions on them as it was, and we were damn loud at times given the warfare we were waging in their country.

Yet, *Stars and Stripes,* which was printed on Japanese rice paper, was a most welcome newspaper in Vietnam. Every day, 61,000 copies were flown in from Tokyo on an Airforce C-130 which landed pre-dawn at Tan Son Nhut. While the newspaper sold for a nickel in the rest of Asia and Europe, it was free for distribution to American soldiers *in country.* Despite the obvious enemy challenges that might pop up at any time, copies were distributed throughout the Mekong Delta, the coastal lowlands, up to the Central Highlands and Da Nang. They were delivered by armored truck, river gunboat, or troop carrier. Sometimes, a helicopter on a mission to bring in extra food or ammunition to a certain combat zone would carry along several hundred copies. As the number of soldiers in the war zone grew, so did the circulation there of *Stars and Stripes*. Combat soldiers could shove a folded copy into the pocket of their jungle jackets for later reading.

Several years after I left Vietnam, I watched on television the evacuation of Saigon in 1975. There on the screen were our Vietnamese friends whose feelings the military hoped we would not offend by pointing our feet in the direction of a shrine, being left behind to face the brutality of the VC. *Stars and Stripes* had warned us that, "It is vitally important that U.S. servicemen make the distinction between the VC and the loyal Vietnamese who make up the overwhelming majority of the people. Careless acts that hurt the people who are innocent civilians endanger the support and loyalty of this group to the legal government and to our military effort."

We *abandoned* those people, our allies, to certain torture and death. So much for respect and loyalty.

The monsoons had begun soon after I arrived at Tan Son Nhut. I hadn't been in-country long when Cholon was hit once again with fierce fighting. On June 18, the largest Communist surrender of the war took place when 152 members of the Quyet Thang, a Viet Cong regiment, surrendered to the ARVN forces. Saigon suffered greatly with 500 citizens killed, nearly 5,000 wounded, and 87,000 made homeless. It was stressful to be living off-base in the midst of such fighting. It was also heart-rending to see families digging in the rubble that had once been that home they respected so highly. And there would be a lot more attacks on the city to come. And yet, life in Saigon went on. Pretty Vietnamese girls still called out to American soldiers as we walked down the streets to, "Please give me GI baby!" A lot of young women learned the hard way that that would not be a sure ticket to the United States.

I hated seeing Vietnamese children living in the wreckage of wartime. With the occasional mortars and gunfire in Saigon, I was reminded of the "Duck and Cover" campaign that was launched in the United States when I was in my first year of school and collecting pop bottles. Typically, throughout our history, the United States didn't worry about the homeland being attacked by a foreign enemy. And then came the Cold War with its threat of a nuclear bomb. In order to prepare America in the event of a bomb being dropped on us by Russia, the Civil Defense program created an animated turtle named Bert. His job was to inform us all what to do, especially schoolchildren.

Along the lines of an Aesop fable, a monkey hangs from a tree and taunts Bert by dangling a lit stick of dynamite over the turtle's head. The wise Bert immediately drops and withdraws into his shell just before an explosion obliterates both the monkey and the tree he's sitting in.

Children of the 1950s and early 1960s learned quickly to "duck and cover." Intent on scaring the daylights out of us all, the Civil Defense sent forth into America a convoy of ten large trucks pulling trailers loaded with posters and brochures of information on what to do during a nuclear attack. The trailers were also mobile theaters that showed the *Duck and Cover* film starring Bert, the wise turtle, and the soon-to-be-killed monkey.

Over a million people walked into those trailers to watch the film. Children learned quickly. Should we hear a warning alarm or see a bright flash, we were drilled to drop to the floor if in school, and roll in under our desks for cover. "Don't run to the window to look at the flash!" our teachers warned us. "The blast wave will arrive next and it will shatter the glass into flying bits. So get under your desks!" All the talk back then was of bomb shelters, and how much food and water should be stored in them for the lucky families who could afford to build one. We kids fell asleep at night wondering what Russia might do as we slept.

Some of the living conditions in Vietnam during the war

And yet, every day I saw the children in Vietnam with no plan at all, no shelter to speak of, no hard shell such as Bert carried on his back. They were living with a downpour of bombs and even napalm. And they were often smiling. They seemed happy just to be alive. The Vietnamese were people who wanted no part of that heinous war. They did everything they could to survive. Children and adults daily scoured the massive dump where the left-overs and unwanted junk of a major army base was discarded. They built the walls of their shacks with pounded out tin cans. They made baskets and sandals and who-knows-what from discarded American rubber tires. They ate our leftovers and made good use of our scraps.

Watching them, I remembered those better days in northern Maine when Dad and I would search the local dump for junk we then turned into treasures in his workshop.

That's where my Red Flyer wagon had come from, and that wagon had made me good money. I often missed my father. I missed the lemon meringue pie my mother made for me on my birthday. I missed home.

During the few days I had off, and they were rare, I met a waitress in Cholon and befriended her. She was Cambodian, slight and pretty. She was waiting hopefully for the American soldier who had gotten her pregnant to come back to Vietnam and marry her.

In the meantime, she worked hard to care for her little girl. Seeing her, she reminded me that I had no girlfriend in my own life. But the friendship between us stayed platonic. I felt she had been jilted by one American soldier already. I did befriend a very poor Vietnamese family. Many such families had daughters who worked as prostitutes to help support their families. They weren't treated with disrespect by their relatives. What they did was a necessity in wartime.

While there was almost no socializing for the WDMET team, Sergeant Flowers became a good ally. He was right that humor would help us endure the daily job. One day, I covered myself with a sheet and lay stiffly on the pathology table, pretending to be a causality as I waited for Dr. Ishler. He was one of the three pathologists on our team. He damn near suffered a heart attack when I sat up suddenly and said, "Hey, Doc. How's it going?" Angry, and probably embarrassed, he wanted me court-martialed. Sergeant Flowers and Major Lane came to my rescue. And yet, I flew off the rails one day when a Vietnamese worker was wearing his hat as he mopped up next to the body of a dead American soldier. He was one of the civilian workers hired to clean up the daily mess from our lab and at the mortuary. "Take off your goddamn hat!" I screamed at him. I felt terrible afterwards, but that was the level of stress we lived with every day. He never made the mistake again, and I appreciated it.

All soldiers a long way from home know those waves of homesickness that can suddenly wash over us. I wrote several letters to Shirley, but there was no reply. I assumed she had moved on with her life.

I did my grocery shopping at the huge **PX** in Cholon and often cooked in my room. The small desk I ate on each night reminded me of the one I had carved information on, to help me memorize facts for my studies in high school. It had been only a few years earlier and yet it seemed like several lifetimes.

While taking X-rays of yet another broken soldier, I would often wonder what the potato farmers were doing back home. I'd imagine the rolling fields filled with small purple stars, the plants all in bloom. Otherwise, I'd have to ask myself yet again why that soldier was on the table in front of me, dead, while I was still alive. Some nights, to help me fall asleep, I'd think of those visits to my grandparents' house in Canada, and all the good French food and music.

Cholon had a fascinating back story about the black market that I soon learned about from Sergeant Flowers. The PX and Commissary store where I shopped was a giant supermarket located at 100 Hung Vuong Street. It was supplied by the Navy Exchange, a retail store chain owned and operated by the U.S. Navy. By 1965, and under the command of Captain Archie Kuntze—he was nicknamed "the American mayor of Saigon—the Cholon commissary had become the largest and most profitable Navy Exchange in the world. It stocked over 1,500 different items in boxes, bottles, and cans, everything from clothing, alcohol, cigarettes, television sets, movie and slide projectors, and stereo equipment. As for food, the store offered 122 varieties of meat products, and 40 kinds of fruits and vegetables.

In 1965 alone, net sales at that one commissary reached almost $9 million dollars. Today, it would be about $72 million. Many of the store's items appeared regularly on the black market, which was thriving in Saigon at that time. It was run by both enlisted and AWOL soldiers. It soon became obvious to military authorities that although there were 200 American nurses serving at that time—in all, there were 700 authorized American women in South Vietnam—the stock for feminine products such as hairspray and cosmetics was outrageously high. While American soldiers often bought those supplies for their Vietnamese girlfriends, it was difficult to explain away 150,000 extra cases of hair spray.

Captain Kuntze was a highly-decorated soldier from World War II and the Korean War. But he ended up in a scandal that would result in a general court martial and his resignation. A colorful character, he often turned up at the site of bombings in full dress whites to direct rescue efforts and talk to reporters. His vehicle of choice in Saigon was a 1964 Buick, the only car in Vietnam with white-walled tires. By sharp contrast, General Westmoreland and his high-ranking staff rode in less conspicuous Chevy sedans.

Making matters worse, Kuntze moved his young Taiwanese girl-friend into his lavish digs and began throwing extravagant parties, all while having a wife back in the States. The investigation into his activities would also reveal an illegal import of Thai silk, needed by the girlfriend's father in his dress shop. Not only was our enemy buying and eating a vast supply of American food bought on Kuntze's black market in Cholon, they were digging with American shovels the network of tunnels used in their guerrilla warfare tactics against our soldiers.

I learned to survive. I had no choice. When there were mortar attacks on Saigon, with flares lighting up the sky, I tried not to think of how easily the billet could suddenly explode in flames. Instead, I remembered the night at Chapman Street when I was about six years old and the house next door to us caught on fire. I had watched from the upstairs window of my bedroom as the building crumbled in fire and smoke. I was terrified that the flames would reach our house and it would disappear beneath me. But it didn't. Everyone got out safely, and the fire trucks came and soon the flames were smoldering in wet ashes. "This is the same thing," I would tell myself when Cholon received another attack. "A mortar won't hit this place. I'll be safe." Some nights, I barely slept. Some mornings, I didn't want to get out of bed. Getting out of bed meant I had to drive my jeep back to the mortuary.

We stayed damn busy with the study. Before we moved to the new facility, members of my team took turns each week keeping the two generators for the trailers running and in good condition. Each morning one of us would start them up. We'd check the oil and the fuel barrels, which held diesel. If the oil needed changing, we did it. At night, we'd shut them down. We couldn't wear earplugs, of course, even though they would have helped with the constant noise from the generators. We needed to communicate with each other in the lab. And then, we were in a war zone. It was a good idea to be able to hear an incoming mortar shell or a rocket.

I had a very small X-ray room when we finally moved into the new facility that September. It had a safe light where I could develop the films. It also became my own quiet place once the job was done. Until I made sure the X-ray had turned out all right, the soldier stayed on my table. There were many times that I had to do the X-ray over. Then the casualty would be wheeled to pathology. Alone again, that small room became a refuge where I could be free for a time, sitting in the dim light and imagining myself half a world away. I developed around 2,500 films during the time I was in Vietnam.

Another job that I actually learned to enjoy when I wasn't X-raying was with the guys who reassembled the bones. They were a unit attached to the mortuary. I'd go out to help them put the bones of fallen soldiers into place. I'd sometimes hum the old spiritual, "Dem Bones." It's the song where the prophet Ezekiel has a vision of standing in the Valley of Dry Bones when suddenly they begin to connect themselves. To keep my mind off the truth behind this work, I'd sing to myself, "Toe bone connected to the foot bone. Foot bone connected to the heel bone." I didn't forget that I was tone deaf, as I had learned while at college. This singing was just for me to hear.

The work reminded me of a special time with my father. One Halloween there was a costume contest held in our town. We decided to enter by creating a robot costume for me to wear. We found a small cardboard box for the head and stapled it to a bigger box for the body. Dad fashioned two pieces of cardboard for the legs and connected them to the body with wire. He fixed a small antenna to the top of the head. The ears were glued-on electrical insulators. The eyes and nose were also insulators, but smaller. We drew a mouth onto the head around an opening Dad had cut. I could look out that opening to see where I was going. We won first prize, a Brownie Kodak camera. "Shoulder bone connected to the neck bone. Neck bone connected to the head bone.

Now hear the word of the Lord."

To help keep our sanity, we listened to the best damn music the world might ever know, the hits songs of the 1960s. *Mr. Tambourine Man. Eve of Destruction. Soul and Inspiration. Light My Fire. Green Green Grass of Home. Whiter Shade of Pale. Mrs. Robinson. Born to be Wild. Midnight Confessions.* At the NCO club, the Vietnamese bands did their best to sing the American hits, but they weren't the Righteous Brothers, or the Beatles, or the Rolling Stones. On a rare night that I went to the club, the band cranked out a shaky rendition of *God Bless America.* I refused to stand up when the other soldiers did. At that point in time, I felt I owed everything to my teammates, and nothing to the American government or the military. They had dropped us into the middle of that damn war as if we were nothing but chess pieces. It was *their* game, not mine. So I refused to stand. Some Marines at the bar noticed and were about to come after me. Sergeant Flowers hurried me out the front door in one piece.

When autumn arrived, I received a letter from my mother telling me that Ginger had died. How do you mourn the loss of a dog amid the deaths of so many fallen soldiers? You save it for when you are home again. I filed that news away in the back of my mind with many other things. Mom's letter was followed by one from my sister Diane telling me that the potato harvest had begun back home. *This* was the type of letter I could live by. I could almost smell the crisp fall air. I imagined the azure skies, the red and orange leaves, the tractors digging up rows of new potatoes, the smell of rich earth, and the excited voices of the pickers as they filled their barrels. The trucks would be loaded and those barrels of potatoes dumped into the waiting railroad cars I remembered so well back on Chapman Street.

Empty Chinooks preparing for next flight

But I was in Vietnam. And above the incoming choppers, above the bombs and the dead bodies, Apollo 7 had become the first human spaceflight mission to send a crew into space, in October 1968. Just two months later, Apollo's second manned mission left earth's orbit and this time circled the moon before coming home again. They were paving the way for Neil Armstrong's "giant leap for mankind" several months later when he walked on the lunar surface. That was the same moon we were looking up at each night from Vietnam, regardless of which side of the planet we were on. Who stepped on it first didn't matter to any of us. We didn't want to go to the moon. We wanted to go *home*. And Eric Burden and the Animals kept on singing, "We gotta get outta this place."

No shit.

Chapter 9

WDMET ENDS—GOING HOME

The young dead soldiers do not speak.

They say: We have given our lives but until it is finished no one can know what our lives gave.
They say: Our deaths are not ours: they are yours, they will mean what you make them.
They say: Whether our lives and our deaths were for peace and a new hope or for nothing we cannot say, it is you who must say this.
We leave you our deaths. Give them their meaning. We were young, they say. We have died; remember us.

"THE YOUNG DEAD SOLDIERS"
by ARCHIBALD MACLEISH

Monsoon season. View from the top of Ray's billet in Saigon

T he rains continued into November. The streets ran with
mud and the wind blew hard from the southwest. In late
December, the wind reversed and came down cold and dry
from China and Siberia, wind that would stay with us until it shifted
again the following May and brought back the sweltering heat. But
those changes would mean that I had become a definite short timer,
that I had spent almost a whole damned year in-country and survived. The return of the hot season would also mean my own return
to the United States, and then northern Maine. But I still had half
a year to go.

After six months in-country, I was eligible for the one R & R
that the military allowed all personnel serving in Vietnam. The
5-day leaves were for closer destinations like Hong Kong, Manila,
and Singapore. The 7-day leaves were for farther distances like
Australia and Hawaii. GIs who weren't married preferred places
like Bangkok, Thailand, known for its many prostitutes who eagerly
welcomed American soldiers. Pattaya Beach, about 60 miles southeast of Bangkok, had a thriving sex industry thanks to Uncle Sam.
Pattaya had been a quiet fishing village until five hundred GIs con-
verged on it in 1959, from the nearby military base at Korat. The
rest was sex history. Married soldiers tended to meet their wives and
families in Hawaii.

I took my leave over the Christmas of 1968. I just wanted to get
as far away from Vietnam as I could. I wanted a nice motel room,
one with a soft bed and a clean bathroom, where no explosions
would be heard during the night. I went to Sydney, Australia, and
did my best to erase the images that were fixed in my mind. But it
wasn't easy. The truth was that I had been introduced to an aspect
of warfare that very few people knew about. Even our fellow soldiers
who slept in the barracks at Tan Son Nhut, or ate in the mess hall,
were mostly unaware that a mortuary sat outside the base perimeter.
And yet, caring for the military dead had been an important, even
moral consideration for many wars throughout history. It's a part

of warfare that deserves recognition. Every politician should know these facts before they send soldiers into battle.

Since World War I, American soldiers who had this job were known as the Graves Registration Service, now called Mortuary Affairs. Those men over history, and those who spent a year at the Tan Son Nhut mortuary, some of them two years, suffered greatly from the job. I was told that one soldier at TSN would go into the freezer unit, close the door, and scream. A few had funerary experience before they joined the military, but most didn't. We wouldn't learn until years later that the PTSD these guys suffered would rank among the highest for veterans. The same was true for most of us on the WDMET team. I spent that Christmas week in Australia, and to this day I have no memory of it, just some slides I took of buildings, statues, and beach scenes that have no meaning to me. But for some reason, I remember that the soldier in the room next to me was robbed by the prostitute he hired. He woke up the next morning with nothing left but the smile on his face.

My respect for the mortuary guys, as well as the unit who sorted over heaps of bones, grew daily. And then, during any war, soldiers don't die just in combat. Of all those names on the wall at the Vietnam Veterans Memorial, over 9,000 died in accidents, which likely included drug overdoses. Over 900 died from illnesses, almost 400 took their own lives, and over 200 were murdered. Eight brave female nurses died in Vietnam. In all, 67 American women were casualties. The Graves Registration guys saw them all. But back home, no one seemed to speak of the two mortuaries.

As I said earlier, the American public knew all about those soldiers coming home from Vietnam in the bellies of cargo planes thanks to the nightly news. But they didn't ask details. I had been studying X-ray technology all those months in Texas, knowing I would likely end up in Vietnam. And yet I thought in terms of medics, and hospitals, and helping the wounded. I also never asked, "Are there mortuaries in Vietnam? How are all those bodies able to come home?" Again, every politician should know what happens behind the scenes. They should be given a tour of a military mortuary at the height of the conflict. It should be a prerequisite for any man or woman who votes on whether or not to take our country into warfare. They might still decide to do it, and they might even be making the right decision. But at least they would be better informed of the consequences.

I never learned back then the names of the men who worked across the hall from where our study was taking place. I probably never even asked. If socializing off-base was limited, it was more so at the mortuary. But I sure as hell came to admire them. In my mind, they were among our unsung heroes. The inscription on the Tomb of the Unknown Soldier in Arlington National Cemetery is "Here rests in honored glory an American soldier known but to God." These guys kept that motto in mind, because they wanted our soldiers who died in Vietnam to be *known* to their families and friends. To the whole damn world. Sadly, there are still soldiers missing on foreign soils wherever we engaged in the theater of battle.

As I endured my year at the mortuary, I became more familiar with how countries handled this circumstance of war over the centuries. Since antiquity, the world's military has cared for causalities as best they could, and when they could. What is believed to be the earliest record of a country bringing its fallen soldiers home was written by the Greek historian Thucydides, in the fifth century BC, regarding soldiers killed during the Peloponnesian War between Athens and Sparta. The Athenian soldiers who fell were cremated on the battlefield, but their bones were brought back to Athens and laid out in tents. For three days, relatives and friends could bring flowers and gifts to say goodbye. The bones were then placed in cypress coffins and buried in flowering gardens.

During our Revolutionary War, Seminole Wars, and Mexican-American War, soldiers were pretty much buried where they fell and anonymously if they were mere foot soldiers. During the Civil War, for the first time, Americans made an effort to identify the dead, making field commanders responsible for the task. But needless to say, with astounding casualties in each battle, their thoughts then were more on victory than burial efforts, let alone identification. It was during the Spanish American War that the United States became the first country in the world to initiate a policy to return soldiers fallen in a foreign theater back to their families when the war was over.

During World War I, and the formation of GRS, our soldiers were buried by individual combat units often in one of several temporary cemeteries until they could be shipped home when the fighting was over. This temporary burial system usually required months and even years. The same was true in World War II. The soldiers would be disinterred and returned home to their families. Or, should the family prefer, they were buried in overseas U.S. cemeteries.

During the Korean War, difficult as it was to rescue casualties from that rugged and hilly terrain, the military began sending soldiers home as soon as possible, which could still be weeks. While nothing could lessen a family's grief over losing a loved one, this system at least brought the soldiers home more quickly than in previous wars. Many families felt the emotional need to view the remains and have a proper funeral. But technology changed everything by the time we were engaged in combat in Southeast Asia. In Vietnam, casualties might be evacuated from the battlefield by helicopters, Hueys or Chinooks, within a couple of hours after death occurred, unless the body was in an inaccessible area and retrieval took days or weeks. They were driven or flown to one of thirty collection points situated around the country. And imagine the soldiers given this task.

From the collection points, things sped up. These collection points had small refrigeration facilities that could hold anywhere from five to twenty bodies. All personal belongings were removed there to be sent to Camp Redball before being mailed back to relatives. Within 24 hours the remains, with paperwork, were flown from the collection point by helicopter or taken by truck to either Tan Son Nhut or Da Nang. Tan Son Nhut had room for 250 bodies at a time, and yet there were so many coming at the height of the war that they were often stacked on top of each other. The mortuary guys stayed busy seven days a week.

Transfer cases with human remains ready to be shipped out

After landing at the TSN helipad, the body bags were then carried into the mortuary within 30 minutes and placed on one of the six embalming tables. In-processing began as the men made sure that all personal items possibly missed at the collection points were removed. Identification was next, hopefully beginning with the name on a shirt, unless the death had been so aggressive that the clothing was gone. Dog tags, scars, and tattoos helped. Dental records were a very reliable source, but took much longer to get back in those days. Fingerprinting accounted for about half of the identifications. Occasionally, when a body was in an advanced state of decomposition and hard to fingerprint, the guys in the mortuary would actually put the loosened skin on their own fingertips so they could make a print. It was staggering to witness. And some of the GRS guys personally did 10,000 embalmings if they were there for two years.

The embalming itself took a little over two hours. After eight hours of holding time for the treatment to take effect, the body was put inside the aluminum transfer case. When a plane was due to arrive on the airstrip, the cases were placed on pallets. Each pallet could hold three cases. They were stacked on top of each other four pallets high for a dozen bodies. The mortuary had its own flatbed truck big enough to carry four pallets at a time. It was all carefully coordinated. As soon as the C-141 or the C-5 Galaxy landed, the truck sped out to the airstrip and the pallets were hurriedly loaded into its belly. It made as many trips out to the plane as was necessary. It happened quickly because the military didn't want the soldiers stationed at Tan Son Nhut to see those cases going home. And then, the heat and humidity required fast movement, even after embalming. Those transfer cases came back to Vietnam from the States for the next bodies. They were too expensive not to recycle.

If all went as planned, in just under thirteen hours, the soldier was on his way home. If home was east of the Mississippi River, casualties went to the mortuary at Dover Airforce Base in Delaware. If home was west of the Mississippi, they went to the mortuary at Travis Airbase in California. At these ports of entry, the remains were reprocessed, which included cosmetics, civilian clothing, or dress uniform. They were then placed in caskets for shipment to a funeral home or cemetery, as requested by the family. A soldier accompanied each casket. If the family asked, he would stay for the funeral. It usually required seven to ten days before the soldier was home again.

The North Vietnamese didn't have this problem. Winning the war was a rung above using manpower and reserves to bury their dead. It was well-known that our enemy's fallen soldiers stayed where they fell. We were told that the biggest problem with the M-16s was that they were killing the enemy. The fine art of wars past indicated that leaving an enemy soldier wounded instead of dead was the better choice. It would require his fellow soldiers to spend valuable time and money in his rescue and rehabilitation. We knew this was ridiculous since the Viet Cong had no means of administering care to the tens of thousands of their wounded men. They didn't have the resources, even if they did have the concern.

The word autopsy is derived from the Greek word *autopsia,* which means "to see with one's own eyes." During my year with the WDMET team we did approximately 800 autopsies. There were busier days than others depending on the number of causalities. Remarkably, during the 4-day period from September 7 to September 10, 1968, we personally conducted 55 autopsies, or almost 14 a day. WOUNDS DATA MUNITIONS EFFECTIVENESS TEAM. The *Wounds Data* part was what was collected in the field and then photographed, X-rayed, and autopsied at the mortuaries. The *Munitions Effectiveness* part was the evaluation that would be done on the two-year study once that mountain of material was shipped back to the United States, to Edgewood Arsenal, in Maryland. That was where the study initially began.

In late February, when I had less than four months to go in Vietnam, Tet 1969 began, with attacks on military bases, and civilian towns and cities, particularly in the south. With Saigon and the surrounding area greatly affected, sleeping in the billet at night became more difficult. Over 1,000 American casualties were counted. I kept doing my job and praying. But I was having horrible dreams at night. In one that was recurring, I stood frozen as dead bodies climbed like zombies down from a helicopter and walked toward me. I'd wake to the sheet soaking wet beneath me and a pounding in my chest. I wasn't sure how much more I could stand. But I had no choice.

Running away was not an option. Just two years earlier, a military jail had been established there, a barbed wire compound that was eight acres in area and capable of housing 400 prisoners. The previous stockade had been at the sports field near Tan Son Nhut Air Base. But the sports field jail could hold only 140 prisoners. With a growing demand for more American soldiers on the ground in Vietnam came the demand for a bigger prison to hold the criminals and malcontents. The crimes they had committed were similar to what you would find in a civilian prison, drug use or trafficking drugs, theft, assault, rape, attempted murder, murder, and going AWOL. Racial tension also existed, as it does in civilian prisons. Depending on the seriousness of the crime, a man might serve his full time at Long Binh, or be shipped back to the States and the penitentiary at Fort Leavenworth, Kansas. When I arrived at Long Binh, the facility housed over 700 men, nearly twice the number it was intended to hold. The 70-square-feet-per-prisoner that the original plans allotted to each man had shrunk down to 36 feet. The LBJ, as it was known, should have been a damned good deterrent. It apparently wasn't.

Three weeks before my tour of duty was up, a battle occurred up north near Da Nang, close to the border with Laos, at a place the Vietnamese called Dong Ap Bia. The U.S. military called it Hill 937, because it was that high in meters. The 101st Airborne Division engaged in intense combat against a North Vietnamese regiment that was entrenched at the top. The battle raged on for ten days with heavy losses. It was a turning point in the war, especially with the American public. Controversial, it would become known as the Battle of Hamburger Hill and was the topic of daily conversation as my time to leave Vietnam drew near. I hoped luck was riding with me and I'd get out of that country alive. I barely did.

An event happened a week before Major Lane and I were scheduled to leave. It would seal the trauma of war for me. We were driving up Plantation Road in the Army Dodge stretch pickup we often used when we traveled as a group. Raynold "Ray" Eaton—a team member with the same first name as me—was driving. Major Lane rode in the rear seat behind the driver, while Sergeant Jim Flowers, the closest friend I had made in Vietnam, and I completed the contingent. Suddenly a motor scooter appeared out of the noisy throng of other vehicles. Scooters greatly outnumbered the old American automobiles in Saigon. I enjoyed watching them compete at a 4-way stop, a dozen piling up as close to the line as possible, waiting for the light to change. When it turned green, they would all shoot forward at once. This scooter was driven by a petite Vietnamese girl. Behind her, arms clutching the driver's slim waist, was another young girl.

Two girls on a moped. This is similar to the girls who threw the satchel charge from their moped into the army truck that Ray was riding back to Saigon in.

The girls had shiny black hair and flawless skin. At first, I thought, "What pretty schoolgirls." When the scooter pulled up next to the truck, I noticed that each girl had a knapsack strapped to her back. That's when a thought formed instantly in my mind: *Is this danger?* We were probably all thinking the same thing at the same time. It wasn't uncommon for the Viet Cong to use young sympathizers to lob grenades at American installations. In fact, it happened often. That January two billets in Saigon had been targeted, and the cafeteria on the base had been bombed by civilian workers.

Before any of us could react, there was an earsplitting explosion. A large chunk of the scooter flew into the air and bounced across the hood. I looked out and up and saw scooter and body parts falling all around us. The satchel charge that had been hidden in the knapsacks, whether dynamite or the more powerful C-4 plastic explosive, had gone off prematurely. Shaken from the realization of what our fate could have been, we stopped at headquarters, gave the required report and continued on to the mortuary work area, where we washed explosion powder, blood, and flesh off parts of the vehicle.

This was the awful irony of war. The deaths of these girls had likely saved our lives. But there was something in seeing those beautiful young faces riding toward us on that scooter, hoping to kill us, that was the final coup de grâce for me. I had a week to go and yet I almost didn't make it.

In early June, 1969, the study officially came to an end. I had served a full year on the team. We used funds in the team's coffers to have a goodbye party. Colonel Ostrom presented me with the Army Commendation Medal. I would learn later that Ostrom wrote a superlative letter recommending me for the Bronze Star, which I was denied. It's possible this decision was made by an officer who had no idea what WDMET was, or what I'd been through. Only a handful of us would know the facts of the study. And the majority of those facts we'd learn years later, by researching on our own. But in the two years since its inception, WDMET had collected and studied 8,000 combat casualty cases. It compiled approximately 200,000 pages of original documents, took over 55,000 colored slides, and filled several filing cabinets with bullets and shrapnel taken from wounds.

Would any good come of it? Who the hell knew back then? Nobody. But I had done my own "study" those many nights that I woke from a nightmare to the sound of explosions, those days of the noisy generators and devastated bodies. And my personal study seemed like a smart one to me. If the military wanted to save future soldiers, it should stop sending them into battle. Then it wouldn't matter one damned bit if vests or helmets were improved. If there were no wars to fight, did it matter what damage bullets or shrapnel could do to the human body? But I knew it was useless to rail against war. War had been a part of humanity since the first rock was thrown, the first arrow shot, the first moat built around a castle.

Colonel Ostrom presented our team with a memento of our service by giving each member a machete made by a Vietnamese Montagnard tribe, the indigenous people from the Central Highlands. That Montagnard is a French word for *mountain man* was indicative of the long-lasting effects of colonialism. As our allies in the fight against communism, the Montagnards had been killed in great numbers, ill-treated and abused, especially during President Diem's "God Has Gone South" campaign when the exodus from North Vietnam to the south passed through Montagnard territory. Inscribed on the sword was this message: *This machete will serve as a reminder of your tour in Vietnam. I hope that it will in some small way show this unit's appreciation for all your dedicated service and hard work. Best wishes for your continued success.*

Ray after he had been in-country for about three months. Not the happy look he had on his face when he first arrived.

After a year in Vietnam, I feared I had lost the foundation of beliefs I had built my entire life upon. Was there really a God? And if there was, WHAT THE HELL WAS HE THINKING? It seemed to me that Colonel Ostrom's motto was a more logical one to live by: "You win a few, you lose a few." A week after our farewell party, my Montagnard machete and I boarded a Boeing 707 bound for the States. As the plane gained altitude, I looked down at the Saigon River twisting its way southeast from Cambodia to curl around the city's eastern border. From there it poured into the South China Sea near the Mekong Delta. The French, in their early exuberance to turn that part of the world into a western outpost, had christened the new settlement at Saigon "the Pearl of the Far East." Then the Boeing entered a cloudbank and that was the last I saw of the country I'd never truly leave behind me.

Some hours later, we landed at Travis Air Force Base and I was taken to the Processing Center in Oakland, California. I was finally discharged and went on to San Francisco for a flight back home. At long last, I was safely back where I belonged. Or was I?

I knew on the long flight home from California to Boston, and then north to Presque Isle, that it would be impossible to step back into the skin of my old life. Leaving South Vietnam for northern Maine was like moving from one hazy dream to another. Nothing seemed real to me anymore. Home was like a foreign planet. I didn't want anyone to meet me at the airport, so I caught a taxi home. Mom had baked me a cake with red, white, and blue frosting. My family was all there, and I smiled in gratitude and made small talk. But I couldn't speak about what I'd been through. I didn't *want* to talk about it. I wanted to forget. I wished Ginger had been there to greet me. We had put a lot of miles under our feet delivering all those papers on the streets of Presque Isle. And Ginger wouldn't have asked questions, just for a pat on the head.

All I remember of those first weeks was sitting in a daze on my mother's front steps and staring at nothing. Dana Bishop, the same mailman who delivered my draft notice, saw me sitting on the steps one day. "You're back, Ray?" he asked, and I nodded. My neighbor across the street, Mrs. Greaves, must have noticed and felt sorry for me.

She had been one of the first neighbors to welcome our family to Academy Street when Dad moved us there. Before I went into the military, I used to see her daughter Sandy, who was a few years behind me in school, walking home with her arms loaded with books. But I didn't know the Greaves family well until Mrs. Greaves started inviting me over for coffee at the kitchen table. Sometimes we sat in rocking chairs on the front porch. I trusted her, but I didn't want to talk about my time in Vietnam. We talked about everything else.

I knew this fog had to lift or it would remain for the rest of my life. I signed up for unemployment benefits, which was about $60 a week. And I did renovations for my mother on her rentals. She asked me to put a second bedroom in a downstairs apartment. She and I seemed to work better together than in our earlier years. Maybe I had learned more patience in the military. Or maybe she decided to cut me some slack, given I'd just returned from the war zone. But I didn't have patience with my younger brother Gary when he tried to help me with the renovation. Poor guy. Nine years old when our father died; he had cried uncontrollably. Now, as a junior in high school, he was probably looking for a role model in his older brother. He wouldn't find it in me that summer. I felt every day that I was living on the edge and ready to jump.

In July, I got a ride over to Silver's Chrysler-Dodge dealership and bought the first car I ever owned. I felt I had earned it. It was a teal-colored Valiant, the premium model loaded with extra chrome, stereo radio, and even air conditioning. This was not my mother's brown Valiant that she had been so protective of a few years earlier. This car was cool. I paid a little over $6,000 cash for it. I felt like a million bucks when I drove it home and parked it next to our house. It had taken a huge chunk out of my savings, so I was relieved when the unemployment office called to say they'd found me a job. I drove my new car over to their office for what the army would have called "a briefing." The woman behind the desk pointed at a huge box on the floor behind her. It was filled with a few dozen tiny boxes of Tide detergent.

"Ray, you can pass these samples out door to door," she said. "When you run out, just come back for some more."

It seems that Tide, the big detergent company, had changed its formula a year earlier for the first time in over two decades. Its new sub-brand would be Tide XK, for "extra cleaning." Apparently, this newsflash needed to go out to the multitude. I don't know why I didn't refuse. Maybe for the same reason I didn't refuse a year earlier when Colonel Ostrom had asked, "Can you handle it, Gauvin?" I had been saving what I could my three years in the army. But I hoped to go to college one day.

And now I had a fancy new car to insure and maintain. Bills were in my future. But it felt like a joke to me after what I'd been through, and all that costly training the military had paid for.

I'd park the Valiant in front of a few houses, grab some samples from the box on my back seat, and then grit my teeth as I walked up to a door and knocked. I prayed no one was home and I could just shove the damn thing into the mail box, or leave it on the welcome mat. When a door did open, I did my best to smile.

"Would you care to try a sample of Tide XK?" I'd ask, falling back on those skills that had sold electric knives and toasters at Zayre's. Sometimes, I knew the woman I was talking to, which made it worse. "It's the very first detergent specially formulated with enzymes to break down those tough protein and carbohydrate stains for a cleaner wash."

It was impossible. I kept remembering the steaming trailers when I first arrived at Tan Son Nhut, of the blood-drenched table and floors, the body bags being hosed down outside by civilians, the goddamned useless loss of life. Now here I was, knocking on doors and talking about enzymes getting stains out of *what?* Towels, white socks, and underwear? I felt degraded and embarrassed. I quit the job after a week and returned to sitting on my mother's front steps. I still didn't know why the pain and the anger wouldn't go away. I didn't know why the zombie dreams continued. I just didn't know back then. The summer wore away like that, with me trying hard to reconnect to the world I'd left behind, and failing.

Finally, I knew something had to give. I had forgotten that I'd sent applications to colleges in Maine while I was still in Saigon. One of those nights in my billet, I guess I sat at the battered desk and filled out forms and addressed envelopes. I was surprised when I was accepted by both the University of Maine in Orono, the main campus, and also the one in Portland. I felt renewed. Maybe the world did have a place for me after all. I'd get back into college and figure out how to prepare a future for myself. As a way of celebration, I went downtown and bought an apricot poodle for Lisa, who was then eight years old. "Every house should have a dog," I told my mother. Lisa had been just two months old when Dad died. She went crazy over the dog and named it Precious.

Mom wasn't pleased at having another dog in the house. But there it was.

I decided on a business degree at the University of Maine in Portland. Many of the local businesses in that city offered internships to the students. That intrigued me. Maybe I'd even start my own business one day. So in August, three weeks after Neil Armstrong stepped on the moon, I loaded the teal Valiant with everything I thought I'd need. I fitted a closet rod across the back seat to hang my shirts and jackets. I bid farewell to family and friends. I made certain to cross the street and say goodbye to Mrs. Greaves. She congratulated me on my new venture. Her daughter, Sandy, had just been accepted at the University of Maine in Orono. "Maybe Sandy can catch a ride home with you now and then," Mrs. Greaves said. I told her I would be happy to drive her.

Interstate 95 had inched north only as far as Augusta then, so it was about an eight-hour drive south. I turned the radio up loud. "Give Peace a Chance" by John Lennon and Yoko Ono was all over the airwaves. It would become one of the most recognized anthems of the anti-war movement. *All we are saying, is give peace a chance.*

I had already agreed to co-rent an efficiency apartment with a guy I knew from home. He had once rented an apartment from my mother and was now working for Coles Express in Portland. He walked me through the place when I arrived. It had a tiny kitchen, two bedrooms, and a small bathroom. It was a clean and safe place, especially since I'd noticed an outside staircase running along the wall. I had always practiced a plan of escape from the billet in Saigon if a mortar rocket hit it one night. This staircase at my new apartment brought me a measure of peace. I unpacked my suitcase, put some books on my desk, and settled down to what I hoped would be a new life. I had done a full year in Vietnam. I had "seen with my own eyes." Now it was time to forget what I'd seen.

Chapter 10

PICKING UP THE PIECES

The brave men and women, who serve their country and, as a result, live constantly with the war inside them, exist in a world of chaos. But the turmoil they experience isn't who they are; the PTSD invades their minds and bodies.

ROBERT KROGER − *Death's Revenge*

The only credits that the University of Maine at Portland would accept from my year at the University of Fredericton were for my class in Logic. I had to start over from the beginning. But I was ready to do that. I settled down to four years of business courses. I got a part-time job as a bag boy at Shaw's Grocery Store and a job in customer service at Bradlees, a discount department store chain. I stocked shelves and waited on customers. There were other Vietnam vets taking courses, but I didn't make friends with them. I think most of us wanted to keep our distance from Vietnam. With school and work there wasn't much time for socializing. I did become friends with a guy my age named John Goodwin, who got married his freshman year. John and I studied together and even made wine using his wife's nylon stockings.

On a couple of the trips I made home to Presque Isle, I stopped at the campus in Orono and picked up Sandy Greaves. I was happy to do this favor for the friendship Mrs. Greaves had shown me. Sandy was very cute, but a little shy. During our rides north together, I got to know her better. We seemed to have a lot in common. But even if I had been ready for a serious relationship, Sandy was five years younger and already had a boyfriend.

I made the dean's list that first semester, despite the time I was putting in at work. It was during my second semester that I got a letter from Sandy. She wrote to tell me that she and her boyfriend had broken up. I had hinted on one of those trips home that I was beginning to like her more than just as a friend. I guess my boldness paid off. I knew Sandy looked up to me as an experienced man of the world. She just didn't know what those "experiences" had been in Vietnam.

We started dating that spring. I took her to a drive-in restaurant and we ordered corn fritters with maple syrup. I don't know if Sandy was nervous, but she spilled her fritters and syrup all over the seat of my prized Valiant. I was so in love by then I didn't care. On another date we drove down to Sand Beach, near Bar Harbor, on a snowy April day. When I drove the Valiant onto the beach and spun its tires around in the sand, it made her laugh. I knew then I was going to marry her.

The big event of the summer of 1970 happened on August 28, near Hanson Lake, while both Sandy and I were back home for a visit. I had taken her to Roma Café for supper and then we drove out to the lake. It was early in the evening of what had been a beautiful summer's day. By the time I snapped open the box the engagement ring sat in, it had begun to rain. That didn't matter to me. I had thought long and hard about this moment. I even sat beneath an oak tree on Munjoy Hill, near my apartment in Portland, running through the pros and cons in my mind. I reminded myself that I had three years of college tuition ahead. Could I afford to get married? And then, Sandy was still only 19 years old. What if a baby came too early? How would we pay those expenses and take on that extra responsibility? In the end, it always came back to Sandy Greaves. We were in love. End of argument.

That early evening at Hanson Lake, with rain beating on the Valiant's roof, I proposed marriage and Sandy accepted. I had never felt so happy in my life. She was the girl I wanted. She was mature for her age. She was intelligent and independent. That was important to me, having seen what my mother faced when she found herself alone in the world. I even liked the way Sandy dressed, stylish and yet unassuming.

Sandy couldn't wait to get home that night and tell her parents the good news.

Then we would cross the street and tell my mother. It was still raining hard as we drove home along the dirt road that was now mud. At a sharp turn, we came upon a car full of young guys who had been drinking. Their car had careened off the road and was stuck on a tree stump. Despite the delay, I had no choice but to stop and pull them out. Our good news would have to wait. Sandy tried to wait patiently in the car, but I could see her constantly shifting position. My shoes and socks were covered in mud before we got their car back on the road. When we reached Academy Street, still excited over our engagement, Sandy's parents weren't home. Her mother, who had rarely gone to a movie in her life, had done just that. Her father was at some meeting. Holding hands, we crossed the street to my mother's house, the same house Dad had been so proud of when he moved his family up to "the hill." We found my mother hunched over the kitchen table, holding a handkerchief. I could tell right away that she was unhappy. It looked as if she had been crying.

"What's wrong?" I asked. Sandy and I exchanged worried looks.

"It's August 28," Mom said. "It's been nine years since we lost your father."

I couldn't believe the day I had chosen to propose to my future wife had been the same day my father had passed away. Was it subliminal? Had I wanted to replicate the partnership I'd had with my father with Sandy? Would my mother be offended if we broke the happy news on such a sad anniversary? I looked at Sandy and could tell she was thinking what I was. *Let's break the good news to our parents tomorrow.*

The following spring, Sandy transferred down to the Gorham campus, near Portland, so we would be closer. We had planned to get married that August anyway. Then we decided there was no reason for Sandy to be in a dorm room and then an apartment when I was close by and also paying rent. Living together was out of the question for both of us, given our backgrounds and our parents. So we moved the wedding up to April 1971. Sandy's mother had already agreed to make her daughter's wedding dress. But she had gone back to college herself and was graduating in late May. She didn't complain, and the dress was beautiful.

Ray and Sandy's wedding picture, April, 1971.

One might take it as an omen that our wedding day was similar to the day we got engaged as far as the weather was concerned. Saturday, April 3, had dawned clear and sunny. By the end of the day, a cold drizzle was falling and a gray fog had moved in over town. But not even that could put a damper on such a happy day in my life. Seeing Sandy in her wedding gown and knowing that we were a young couple with a bright future ahead of us was all that mattered. The Gauvin family and the Greaves family, having lived across Academy Street from each other for over a dozen years, were now packed into St. Mary's Church. This was the church where I had been an altar boy, and also where my father's funeral service was held. That only made me feel closer to him on such an important day that he was missing.

Sandy had dropped out of college until I finished, and now we both had jobs we needed to get back to. We left northern Maine after the wedding and headed down to Portland. The rain, drizzle, and fog followed us south. We checked into a Howard Johnson in Bangor for the night. It would be a decade before we took a real honeymoon. But all that mattered was that we were together.

That autumn, Sandy told me she was pregnant. I had thought she was taking birth control pills. But news reports of the day were cautioning against it, stating that the pill could cause blood clots. This had frightened her, so she had quit taking them and hadn't dared to tell me. With two years of college tuition still to go, and with the pressure of studying while holding down two jobs, I had a reaction that would soon become routine in our lives. Furious with her for misleading me, I stormed out of the apartment and slammed the door behind me. I physically could not carry a third job. How was I going to pay for a baby when we were already living paycheck to paycheck? Here was a cog thrown into the machine I didn't expect. I believed in planning. I had learned that from my father. But now I had gone from wanting to plan to needing control over both Sandy's and my lives.

When I had time to really think of fatherhood, it became an exciting reality to me. I told Sandy, we'd find a way to make it work, we just needed a bigger place. That was when we decided to buy a mobile home. There was a new trailer park in South Windham, only about 15 miles from Portland. We settled into what felt like our first real home. I landscaped around the trailer and added a deck. We bought a yellow VW bug that I adored so much I didn't miss the Valiant. Sandy was learning to cook and it seemed like spaghetti and meatballs in those days was high cuisine. We ate on the coffee table in our tiny living room by candlelight. We made friends with our neighbors. Life was good.

Despite this, Sandy casually mentioned one day that I was moody at times. She was doing all she could to help make our payments. By then she was a teacher's aide with a salary of $55 a week. In those days, that income meant a lot. But I was becoming more short-tempered and I knew it. I was still having the zombie dreams, although I never told Sandy. I didn't know how to talk to her about Vietnam. I didn't know how to talk to anyone. I didn't even talk to *myself.* I wanted to forget that damned mortuary and the war, which was still going on without any sign of letting up.

The famous icebox that came home on top of Ray's Volkswagen Beetle

With the continued stress of school and finances, I became even thriftier than I already had been. I'd complain that we should cut back on food expenses, or maybe eliminate that occasional bottle of wine with those spaghetti dinners. Sandy must have been overwhelmed. She was still just 20 years old and now expecting a baby. I drove into the yard one day with an antique wooden icebox tied to the top of the yellow bug. I unloaded it and carried it into the kitchen. With Sandy watching cautiously, I put it down on the kitchen floor.

"What is that, Ray?" she asked.

"Our new refrigerator."

"You can't be serious," Sandy said.

"We need to cut back on our electric bill," I told her. "This icebox only cost me fifty dollars. It'll last us for years."

I had always liked finding certain antiques, another trait acquired from my father.

I expected the girl who had laughed on our date when I spun the Valiant around in the sand to enjoy the joke. But instead of laughing, Sandy burst into tears and ran into the bedroom.

"Sandy!" I shouted after her. "I was just kidding!"

Maybe it was a signal that my wife was sensing a change in my personality, a subtle, controlling element that was evolving. I came home one day to find Sandy ill with the flu. Pregnant, she had stayed in bed and ignored the dirty dishes in the kitchen sink. I flew into a rage, screaming and shouting at her. That might have been the perfect time for my wife to pack up and leave the marriage. But she stayed. She didn't know what lay ahead.

At the beginning of my junior year, I moved into my major courses of accounting, which was exciting for me. I knew my father would be proud. That next semester, our daughter Michele was born, on May 28, 1972. Sandy's mother came down for a week to help us out. I fell in love with the little girl with the dark curly hair and big brown eyes. Without consciously knowing it, my job was to protect that baby and her mother from danger, real or imagined. It no longer mattered that I was in Maine, not Vietnam. I remember one day, though, that it was real. We needed a second car since Sandy had her job. And she had household errands to run. So we bought a green Ford Pinto. It made quite a visual sitting next to the yellow VW at the trailer park. Just as I once had problems backing up and parking on hillsides, Sandy now had trouble learning to drive a standard shift.

One day she called me at work. She was hysterical and calling from a stranger's house. She had been on her way home with groceries, following behind an oil truck.

Michele was in her car seat in the back. When the truck missed a turn-off, it backed up, not seeing the Pinto behind. Sandy blew the horn but the driver didn't hear it. With the truck still inching backward, Sandy jumped from her car and ran to his window.

"You're backing over my car!" she screamed. By this time, he'd pushed the front of the Pinto down to the pavement as though it were tinfoil. Our little girl was still in her car seat. Sandy asked to use the phone in a nearby house and called me. I don't remember how many red lights I ignored as I hurried to the address she gave me. When I arrived, she was smoking a cigarette someone had given her. Her hands were shaking so badly she could hardly hold it. Sandy had never smoked before, and she never did again. That's how upset she was thinking that Michele had almost not made it.

After the police came and did a report, I drove her and the baby home. All I could think of was that I had not protected my family. I didn't remind myself that I couldn't be with them all the time. That didn't matter. It was my job to look out for them. At those times of fear and stress, I'd think of those schoolgirls on the motorbike who hoped to kill me and my team members my last week in Saigon. I even felt guilt that I hadn't been able to save *them*. They were just little girls, after all. Back at home, Sandy poured herself a strong drink while I put Michele in her crib. I knew then I would have to be more vigilant. My wife and child had been in danger and where had I been? I'd been at my job at the medical center. I had failed them. I was a lousy husband and father. These feelings were signs, but I just didn't know how to read them then.

I made it to my senior year. On my days off from school and work, with Sandy at her job, I'd put Michele in a carrier on my back and take her down to the lake behind the trailer park. One winter's day, I bent to avoid a low-hanging branch laden with snow.

Gladys, Ray, and Lisa the day of Ray's college graduation

Michele, still barely a year old, went flying over my head and landed in a foot of snow. I was lucky and I learned to be more cautious. But what was more serious now with our little girl was that we began noticing she was exhibiting unusual behaviors. If we took her to other houses to visit friends, she had to touch everything, her little hands reaching for a flower vase or books on a shelf, or breaking glass items sitting on a coffee table. It seemed more than just a toddler being a toddler. We were so embarrassed that we hated to take her to visit anyone. We would not learn until much later that Michele had weak eye muscles. Kids with that kind of vision disorder touch things to try and understand what the object looks like. We later learned that she also had Attention Deficit Disorder.

I graduated in May of 1973. My mother and sister Lisa drove down for my graduation. One significant event that stands out on that happy occasion was most personal to me. A teacher I had back in the eighth grade was also there that day, graduating with a master's degree. I went to find him when the ceremony was over. I had something to say to him. "I was in your home room class at Cunningham Junior High." He didn't recognize me, but I certainly

Ray at his graduation from The University of Maine at Portland

remembered him. This was the man who had said to me in front of everyone, "Raynold, you are so stupid that you'll never make anything of yourself." I reminded him of what he had predicted. Since I was wearing my college cap and gown it was obvious he'd been wrong. All he said was, "Oh?" Then he turned and walked away.

I got a job with an accounting firm so things were looking good financially. We should have been relieved, but my relationship with Sandy had grown rockier.

I was losing my temper more and more often. I was impatient with her over the smallest issues. It probably wasn't the best time to think of buying a house, which is usually a stressful endeavor in itself. We found a small one in Falmouth, about ten miles north of Portland. In my spare time, I began renovations, despite the FHA paperwork not being finalized. The biggest problem I faced was in digging a new well. The company I hired drilled three different holes with no luck.

It was during this time that I was let go from my job when the firm merged with a larger, national one. Having been there just 13 months, I was the last hired and first to be cut. It was understandable, but I took it personally. It spelled failure to me. Shortly after this, it became clear that we wouldn't get the loan for our new house. It went back to the FHA. All the time and expense in renovations I'd done on that house went down the drain. That was the litmus test for me. When I began to seek privacy to release my fits of anger, I knew that something was seriously wrong.

I also began wavering on what my future vocation might be. In 1974, I even took a civil service test. When I did well on it, I interviewed with the United States Border Patrol. They saw my background in the military, and especially service in Vietnam, as helpful to the job and offered me an assignment on our southern border with Mexico.

When they referred to it as a "combat zone," I politely refused. I'd already done my time, as I saw it. I accepted a job with another accounting firm instead and moved Sandy and Michele up to Bangor. We bought a mobile home in a safe park and settled in. We were lucky in that we found a reliable babysitter just a few doors down from us, a friendly older couple who were terrific with Michele. Sandy was able to get a job in customer service at Sears.

One morning she called me. She had been too ill to go to work and had passed out and hit her head on a bookshelf. Her forehead was bleeding. I raced her to the hospital and she passed out in the emergency room. I was terrified I was going to lose her. The doctor told us that she was pregnant. This was an ectopic pregnancy, when the fertilized egg attaches itself to the fallopian tube rather than the lining of the uterus. Sandy underwent surgery. Because she had to remain a few days in the hospital, her parents came down and got Michele for a week. It was times like that when I felt the largest amount of guilt. I remembered how I had lost patience with Sandy over nothing important. I had insisted, for instance, that she take over our finances since I was too busy with work. Inexperienced, she had a terrible time keeping track of things, and I gave her no help. I kept telling myself that my bad temper was over now. If I couldn't be an ideal husband, I'd be a good one. I made that same promise to myself many times.

It was hard to put the war behind me when it was still going on. All through my marriage and school years, it was just a television newscast away. The newspapers were filled with it. Then in April, the city of Saigon fell to the Viet Cong and the People's Army of North Vietnam. To the north, Da Nang had already fallen. Fearing a bloodbath, the evacuation of American civilians had begun a month earlier, including "at risk" Vietnamese, those people who had been our friends.

American embassies began to empty. Many Americans were told they couldn't take their common-law Vietnamese wives and children with them. The American public watched as innocent people scrambled to board helicopters. The more prosperous South Vietnamese sold what they owned and bought their way out of the country when they could. Those less fortunate could only beg. Operation Babylift evacuated a few thousand orphans.

On April 29, two American soldiers acting as security guards were killed when one of those rockets I feared during my year in the billet struck near the MACV compound in Tan Son Nhut. They were a young corporal from Massachusetts, not yet 22 years old, who had arrived in the country just 11 days earlier. And a 19-year-old Lance Corporal from Iowa, who had been there less than two months. They were the last American soldiers to die in Vietnam. The next day, on April 30, the People's Army of Vietnam raised their flag over the presidential palace.

The Vietnam War was finally over. My own personal war was just revving up.

While Sandy had been recuperating in the hospital, the gods that be at Sears filled her job. There was no other to be had in that department, so she was out of work. Not long after this, I was let go from the CPA firm where I was employed. I couldn't blame it on anything this time but my own bad temperament. I just couldn't get along with my co-workers. I was impatient with them and quick to criticize if I thought something could have been done better. With what seemed like failures piling up, I decided the time had come to rethink my future. I had done my best when I was on my own, whether it was delivering newspapers or selling pop and candy bars from my wagon. I had been a young entrepreneur back then, and I had been successful. I told Sandy that I needed to go back to the beginning, to my roots. I didn't want to work for anyone else.

"I'd like to move home," I said. "Would you be agreeable to that?"

"But you have no job," Sandy said. "And no prospects for one in northern Maine."

"I know," I said. I was thinking of what little prospects all those Vietnamese innocents who had been our allies and friends now had.

"We have no place to live up there." She was right about that, too.

"And we're broke, Ray," Sandy added. And then she asked, "When do you want to leave?"

I had always seen the logic in a good business plan. This time I had none. When we arrived back on Academy Street to live in the basement of her parents' home, I had no idea of the depression that was waiting for me. I found myself lying on the Greaves' sofa in their living room, day after day, with no interest in bettering my situation. Sometimes I'd go to the window, lift back the curtain and watch the Gauvin family carrying on with their lives across the street. I tried to remember my own years growing up in that house. But I felt like a stranger to everyone I knew. It was as if I'd fallen into a hole so dark and deep that no one would ever find me. Once again, Sandy's mother came to my rescue.

This time she didn't play the understanding friend role. Her role now was as my wife's mother, and she saw what my actions were doing to her daughter and grandchild.

"You need to stop feeling sorry for yourself, Ray," she said. "I don't know what you went through in Vietnam, I'm just sorry you did. But now you have a wife and a child to support. Get off my sofa and get your life back."

No one knew what PTSD was back then. So, I picked myself up and went back to work. In no time I had a job with a local insurance company and began training under a good friend to my father-in-law. Sandy's parents were kind enough to let us move into the camp they owned at Portage Lake, less than an hour's drive from town, until we were back on our feet. Since we had only the Pinto left by this time, I hated leaving Sandy and the baby alone at the lake. But we had no choice. We considered ourselves lucky to have another chance to plan our future. There were a lot of blameless people in the world with no home at all.

Another awakening in my life that summer was when I attended my 10th high school reunion. So many of my former classmates had good jobs and owned nice homes. They and their families were enjoying what many would consider the good life. I thought of how supporting his family had been number one in my father's life. It was time for me to get a plan and get going on my own. No more back-peddling as I had been doing.

Many of my classmates were active in local and state organizations. That was an incentive for me to do the same thing. Sandy wanted to go back to college that coming fall. She had put her own education off to help our new family and it was now her turn. Ever since she was a little girl, she had always wanted to be a school teacher. I knew she'd be a good one.

By the end of that summer, and like perpetual gypsies, we moved back to Academy Street and into one of my mother's apartments. I set up a little office in the entryway. Sandy became my secretary, in addition to caring for Michele and continuing with her college courses. My mother didn't like the fact that I had been an accountant like my father, but was now selling insurance. She saw it as a demotion. I was again a failure in my mother's eyes. I thought of reminding her how my father had gone from airline mechanic, to selling vacuum cleaners and Fuller Brush, to carpenter, before he settled into accounting. What was most important to me at that point in time was that I was supporting my family as best I could. I had left the Greaves' s sofa.

In the fall of 1976, Sandy announced that she was pregnant again. We had wanted to have a second child before Michele was much older, but it hadn't happened. This was a surprise that was happily welcomed even though it meant that Sandy would be doing her student teaching the following spring while very pregnant. I liked to tease her that the only C she got was that last semester when she took Teaching Physical Education. At eight months pregnant she couldn't do the forward roll that her classmates could. Why the professor didn't take that into consideration is another one of those mysteries of the universe.

I had followed through on my plans and gotten involved with the Maine State Jaycees. I was chairing their annual convention one morning when Sandy called me to drive her to the hospital. Our son, Christopher Michael, was born that evening, April 16. Sandy graduated from college a month later.

This was a happy time in our family for sure. But around this same time, we hit another tough wall that we didn't expect. Our babysitter noticed some unusual behavior that Michele was displaying. She just wasn't learning at the rate of other kids her age.

Since the babysitter had a degree in early childhood education, we valued her opinion. When Michele was screened for kindergarten, there were developmental delays that showed up in the testing. At the end of her first year, it was recommended that she repeat kindergarten. This hit me hard as a father. I remembered my own early school years, the bullying, my shyness, my feeling intellectually inferior. I had also been kept back that same year. No father wants to see conflict and struggle in his child's future. Sandy and I vowed to be on our guard where Michele was concerned. Sandy's own teaching experience would now come in handy.

We had no inkling then that our greatest battle would be in dealing with those in charge of teaching our daughter. During the year she repeated kindergarten, it was recommended that Michele be tested for special education, which would end up taking two years. We felt we had no choice. We wanted what was best for our little girl. When Michele qualified for the special needs classes, I discovered that her teacher was working with her inside a small cubicle in the classroom that was meant to be a closet. The school had no preparations at that time to teach Special Ed children. I had been working hard on controlling my temper and this situation put it to the test. I wrote a letter to the superintendent. I hadn't forgotten the one who came to Chapman Street to tell my parents to stop speaking French to their children. I had no intention of letting another well-educated man intimidate me. If Michele wasn't taken out of that cubicle and put in a regular classroom, I would contact the Maine Secretary of Education.

That solved the problem. But you have to wonder how many kids were lost in the system because their parents didn't know how to fight back, or maybe didn't care.

Sometimes it seems like it all comes full circle. In the summer of 1977, nearly two decades after my father moved us to "the hill," I bought the old house on Chapman Street and moved my family back to where I had started. I quickly renovated one of the apartments for us to live in. Sandy was unable to find a teaching job that year so she began babysitting the daughter of a friend. Now she had two young babies to tend. I was still working in insurance, back on the street where I had walked through the culvert under the train tracks. That's when I'd see the empty vanilla bottles and Sterno cans left by the potato house and railroad workers, and what my mother called "the fair people." The brook that ran through that culvert was still flooding nearby homes every spring. Now that I was back as an adult, I decided to remedy the situation. I became spokesperson for the street in petitioning the city to build a dike. A year later, it was built. No more flooding in "the French ghetto."

It was on Chapman Street that I had been a boy who dreamed of becoming an entrepreneur. I wanted to own and operate my own business. I felt as if I'd finally come home to face my future.

Chapter 11

THE LONG, DARK ROAD
TO SUCCESS

"When, not if, *you are successful, help the generations coming behind you."*

—MOTTO OF AROOSTOOK ASPIRATIONS INITIATIVE

For the next few years, we adjusted to the changes in our lives. The children were doing well and were healthy and happy. The year after we moved to Chapman Street, Sandy had begun teaching special education. We were able to put most of her salary in the bank. I even started delving into real estate development. We were finally getting ahead financially. Three years later, we bought a small, ranch-style home on Hanson Lake, in the nearby town of Mapleton. The owner was being transferred and had to sell quickly, so we made a good deal on the purchase. Over Labor Day weekend, we moved our furniture and belongings into what was essentially our first real house as a family. We began adding on to it and doing extensive landscaping. It would become the home where we raised our children.

The purchase of our house went well enough that Sandy and I got interested in real estate together. We bought apartments and began to flip houses. I had to find the hours in my spare time to do all the renovations myself. But that was something I'd begun doing at a young age under my father's guidance. One rental property we bought was registered in Sandy's name. When the listing was posted in the local paper, "Sandra Gauvin" was named as the property's owner. When the school principal read this, she called Sandy into her office and closed the door so they could talk privately. "Are you and Ray getting a divorce?" she asked. It was still unusual for women even in the late 1970s to be property owners. This is what my mother had faced those years after my father's death.

Other changes happened in the family. In April 1979, my grand-father Fred Gauvin passed away at the age of eighty-nine. He had represented so many happy times in my childhood. I could never forget the exciting visits to his and Grammie's little house in Canada, just across the international bridge. Those were the early days of kerosene lamps and Grammie's spinning wheel in the summer kitchen. I still had plenty of Gauvin relatives there, but it was as if Grampie Gauvin's death was the last break with my French heritage. My children would know it even less.

I was doing well enough selling insurance that I earned a trip in 1981 to a conference in the Bahamas. Sandy came with me and we considered it our honeymoon, just a decade late. With my sister Lisa now grown and gone from the house on Academy Street, my mother felt she could concentrate on her own life. In the spring of 1982, she married a family friend, a widower. We seemed to all be moving ahead with our lives. But there were times when I'd hear the sound of a helicopter overhead and be reminded of the helipad near the mortuary in Saigon. I avoided wakes and funerals with their perfumed flowers and the slight smell of embalming fluids. Even the odor of disinfectants in a hospital reminded me of formaldehyde. I did my best to concentrate on the future. Things were going well. I had to remember that.

While selling insurance I nonetheless was becoming slowly involved with financial planning. In a nutshell, it's a process with many different elements tailored to suit the needs of couples and individuals in regards to their financial futures. In December of

1969, while I was at Tan Son Nhut anxious for my first leave to Australia, a group of thirteen men met in a room at O'Hare airport in Chicago. Called together and inspired by a successful salesman named Loren Dunton, these men would begin mapping out just what financial planning might involve. Dunton felt the time had come for concerned business people and lay people alike to take control of their financial futures. Otherwise, they would have to depend upon the whims of an unpredictable economy. In addition, he realized that most Americans still did not plan for their retirements.

Word of this new concept slowly began to spread, especially to businesses.

Dunton published the first *Financial Planner* magazine and founded a college. But it was still a new idea to most Americans, and particularly in rural areas. It seemed custom-designed for what I was looking to do, given my own background in business and accounting. In 1984, I started the Center for Financial Planning. I hired Heidi Pelkey Graham, a shy but very bright nineteen-year-old. Heidi had graduated from a local institute with a degree in business, but she had no actual office experience. A year later, I became a

Heidi Graham, Ray's partner in Advantage Payroll Services

registered financial planner. It would be a slow concept to sell to northern Mainers, but I felt it would have a strong future, given time and patience.

That same year I bought my first franchise of Advantage Payroll, founded by a man named Tom Hackett, who would soon become my mentor and good friend. At first, I let Heidi attend to the payroll business so I could concentrate on financial planning. I helped my clients manage the budgets they already had in place, or created new ones for them. We anticipated college tuition for their kids and prepared for their retirements. I sometimes oversaw their portfolios. The business grew slowly and I made good money.

But Tom encouraged me to concentrate more fully on the payroll business. As he saw it, and I soon agreed, Advantage Payroll was the way of the future for companies large and small. An automated payroll system allows an employer to process the company payroll through a computerized system. It was an alternative to having the payroll done manually, processed by in-house employees. That was a considerably slower and more complicated procedure than auto-mation. A manual payroll system also required computing the time clock data by hand, which increased the likelihood of errors.

I was lucky that I had experience with computers from my college days at the University of Maine in Portland. The accounting classes I took solved problems using large IBM mainframes, which were then state of the art. They were larger and had more processing power for bulk data. Computers were on the cusp of changing more than just the financial world. Tom Hackett had advised me well. In no time, I doubled my salary. In the summer of 1985, when I attended my 20th high school reunion, I did so with pride, knowing how far I'd come in a decade. The financial side of things was pro-gressing nicely, but there were downfalls. For every good day I had, I learned to expect there would come a bad day.

Heidi Graham soon realized that she had a mercurial boss to deal with. She was doing her job well. She had overcome her shyness enough to interact confidently with clients and oversee the other female employees I'd hired to work in the office. She soon excelled at marketing tools and procedures. Our clients grew to love her. But if one small thing went amiss, my mood could change on a dime. If someone in the office forgot to do something I'd asked for, or did it incorrectly, I often became impatient, even irate. I might ask an employee to step into my office where I could raise my voice in anger. It was all about controlling my environment. There was a safety in that, as I would come to realize years later.

For my employees, it must have made their work days unpleasant much of the time. They never knew when I'd explode. When I came into the office, I'd see them glance up quickly to determine what kind of expression was on my face. Later, remorseful, I would try to make up for my mood swings and the bouts of anger. I'd compliment them on their work. I'd take them out for a nice lunch. I bought flowers on their birthdays and sometimes arranged a company dinner at a local restaurant. The next day, they might glance up from their desks to see anger on my face as I entered the office.

This was also happening at home. Sandy and the kids never knew what might set me off. We could be having the best time at a park, or restaurant, or playing a game around the kitchen table when I would do a complete 180-degree change. Then the rest of our night was ruined. Our daughter, Michele, was still struggling with learning issues and what we would only discover years later was a mild form of autism. She did many things very well, but at other times she seemed not to listen as we spoke to her. She often didn't make eye contact during conversations. We sometimes had to say her name several times before she responded. Sandy and I assumed it was related to her early developmental delays. But it sometimes felt to me that she was being downright rebellious. I often lost my patience if Michele didn't perform up to my standards. It would trigger my need for people to behave predictably or to act in ways that made me feel safe and in control. I was still in the dark about PTSD and didn't know that these were symptoms of a disorder caused by the trauma I had experienced in Vietnam. It was a strained relationship for us both, and we had no idea why.

It helped that our family stayed very busy. Sandy and I were involved with the local Jaycees and also with our church and other civic activities. Our son was active in Boy Scouts, just as I had been. I enjoyed working with him on the Pinewood Derby that the scouts

Ray's getaway - his camp at Fish Lake.

organized each year. I would take Michele fishing to Hanson Lake. It wasn't that we didn't have good times together. We did. The family went on trips to Bar Harbor every Labor Day and Memorial Day. We went twice to Disney World. But my wife and kids never knew when that fun day was going to turn into my

withdrawing from them. I might refuse to smile or even speak. I finally bought a camp at Fish Lake as a getaway when I felt the walls closing in. But alone there, surrounded by lake and trees, my thoughts sometimes grew darker, even suicidal. My nights were still troubled by those recurring dreams. Sandy said to me one day, "I'm worried about you. These mood swings are getting worse."

One evening in 1987, after having dinner with friends, Sandy told me she wanted a divorce. My behavior was hard for her to deal with, but she was now more worried about the effect it was having on our children. "Ray, I think it would be best for you to leave," she said. I couldn't believe what I was hearing. Of all the pitfalls I had guarded against, divorce had never been one of them. I suddenly felt sharp pains in my chest and had difficulty breathing. My heart racing, I tried to persuade her to change her mind. But I had trouble even speaking. Sandy later said that I wasn't being coherent and that's why she called an ambulance to take me to the emergency clinic. My blood pressure had sky-rocketed, and I was told by the doctor that I had had a mild heart attack. It was late by the time Sandy drove me back home. After she saw me into bed for the night, she went to her parents' house, where the children were. It was a rude awakening to find myself alone inside a quiet house.

I was lucky that I had a forgiving and caring wife. Not all Vietnam veterans can say that. I promised Sandy that things would change if she dropped the idea of divorce. I asked for another chance. I would work hard on my mood swings. Of course, that's a promise often made in these situations, and often broken. I didn't realize then that I needed professional help before I could actually change. But things *were* better for a time. I cut back on some of the business strain I was under by selling the Center for Financial Planning the following year. It was stressful to deal with other people's finances, especially if an investment didn't go as well as I had hoped.

From then on, I concentrated more fully on the Advantage Payroll Services franchise I had bought. Heidi had been doing an excellent job, but I felt I could now take the company to a new level. We continued to grow and I soon realized that this was the business arena where my greatest success could be waiting. Early mornings, often before the sun came up, I'd be on the phone with Tom Hackett as we discussed new ideas for the field. Just as things were looking up, I was diagnosed that same year with type 2 diabetes. I was advised to control my blood sugars with exercise and diet. I did my best to obey those instructions. But oral medication and insulin would be waiting down the road for me.

It would be over a decade later that the Institute of Medicine would conclude that there was evidence of a connection between exposure to herbicides such as Agent Orange and type 2 diabetes. I remembered those drums used for the toilets at Long Binh that I had pulled out of the ground to clean. But mostly, I thought of the drums on the roof of my billet in Saigon with the orange stripes around them. That's where I had taken my daily showers. "Get your *mamma-san* to fill the drums with water each day," the company clerk had told me. "The sunlight will heat it." When my long day at the mortuary was over, I had tiredly climbed the stairs to the roof and stood beneath the shower of water cascading down from those drums.

There were bright moments. My relationship with my mother over the years had grown much better. She would often ask me for financial advice in handling her affairs. She wanted her finances kept separate from her husband's. She even went so far as to put into writing that, should she become incapacitated in her later years, as her oldest son, I would oversee her care. We still had our differences, of course, having met and fought our own obstacles over the years. We were both individuals, but we were coming together again as mother and son. I still had much admiration for how she had maintained herself and the family after my father's death. When she retired, I felt a great satisfaction that I could buy her a house in Florida. My sister was living there, so she'd have family nearby. She could escape those long, cold northern Maine winters.

When my and Sandy's 25th wedding anniversary arrived in April of 1996, our children and Sandy's parents threw a surprise party for us. It was held at my in-laws' home and a dozen friends and family members attended. It was such a relief to enjoy the evening as I did, chatting with our guests. For some time, I had been avoiding social situations, not knowing when I might feel overwhelmed with anxiety. But that night was all about the good part of our lives. The kids had raided the family photo albums and made a CD to celebrate our life together. It began with our wedding day and followed us over the years. Our faces were full of the future. Sandy commented on this later that night as we got ready for bed. "We looked so happy in those pictures, Ray," she said. "No one would ever know about the down times."

By now business was exploding. It was doing so well that I was able to expand. In 1997, I began buying franchises for Advantage Payroll Services in other states. I finally owned ones in New Hampshire, Massachusetts, and Vermont. But that meant a lot of traveling for me and being away from Sandy and the kids. I'd find myself on the road in the dark of night, or when the sun was just coming up. Much of that time driving was on automatic pilot while my conscious mind went over things I needed to do the next day. I was growing more exhausted and stressed as the days wore on. When an employee quit one day without notice at my Vermont franchise, I left northern Maine at 3 am and arrived in Burlington at noon to get out the payroll. After I ate my supper, I drove back home, arriving pre-dawn and about 24 hours later. What I didn't know then was that Sandy and the children were relieved that I was on the road so much. It meant peace in our home.

I needed recharging. I had grown up a county kid. I remembered the long bike rides I'd take to visit my grandparents in Van Buren. I'd ride through fields of freshly cut hay, or through miles thick with the smell of pine trees. I had learned young that nature could be a healer. Being in the outdoors helped me cope with my darkest thoughts. When I found time, I'd drive the hour and a half to my camp at Fish Lake, especially in the spring when my maple trees could be tapped. I wasn't into hobbies like tennis or shooting baskets on the court with a friend. I needed a hobby where I could see that I was accomplishing something, just like those cedar chests and radios I built back in high school. I put 50 taps on my trees at the lake that produced about ten gallons of syrup each season. Making syrup from the sap of a maple tree—it takes 40 gallons of sap to make a single gallon of syrup—and pouring it into bottles for family and friends was a satisfying reward.

I was at my camp doing repairs one Sunday morning when I looked up to see Sandy driving down the dirt road. I knew something important had happened and it would not likely be good news. It wasn't. Tom Hackett, the founder of Advantage Payroll, the man who had become a close friend and personal mentor to me, the man who had steered my career in the right direction, had passed away of a heart attack. He and his wife had been hiking when it happened. I felt this loss greatly. Tom had been on the other end of the phone line all those early mornings when we discussed ideas. He was just in his early 50s and had so much life ahead, not to mention a comfortable retirement that he had earned. I would miss his friendship even more than his mentorship.

It probably shouldn't have been a surprise when I was diagnosed in 1998 with high blood pressure, but it was anyway. I knew I had to stop and smell the roses as the old cliché goes. I began to think of downsizing my businesses. Otherwise, I was going to miss a good part of my life, and important times with my family. By 2000, I had sold all of my out-of-state franchises of Advantage Payroll Services. Now Heidi and I could concentrate on the company in Presque Isle. And Sandy and I could begin a long-held dream of ours by getting involved in philanthropic causes beyond donating money each year to charitable organizations. We wanted a more personal and hands-on involvement.

The same year I sold my franchises, we formed the Gauvin Lighthouse Fund, followed by the Gauvin Family Scholarship. The latter was a scholarship given to seniors from Presque Isle High School whose plans were to attend local colleges in Aroostook County. This was the same high school that Sandy and I had attended. Over the next decade, we allocated approximately $100,000 to a hundred students whose family incomes could use some help with tuition, just as I had needed it. I never forgot those early days on Chapman Street and later on, after my father died. I had been helped with scholarships and mentoring. Now it was time to give that same support back to the young people who would inherit and shape the future of Maine, and possibly the country. I knew my father would be proud of this. Our mentoring began to grow.

In 2002, I bought 85 acres of beautiful land covered in sugar maple trees. It was only a few miles away from our house on Hanson Lake, so easier to get to. I soon began building a beautiful camp there—we called it the Sugar Lodge—that would take me two years to complete. Although the sap of all maple trees contain sugar, it's usually the sugar or rock maple that is tapped. In the autumns, with those maple leaves turning from yellow to bright reds and deep scarlets, this was my own little paradise. Each spring, I put in about 650 taps. Now instead of 10 gallons that I had made at my previous camp, I was able to produce about 80 gallons or more. My clients and friends often went home with a couple of bottles. But what had begun as an enjoyable hobby soon turned into a time-consuming chore. I still didn't realize that by keeping busy I could avoid asking myself what was causing the mood swings and occasional nightmares.

Our daughter was going through difficulties with a young man she had dated and later married. I wasn't too fond of my son-in-law, and my attitude could turn dark in a second when he came around. Thankfully, Michele decided it was time to ask for a divorce. In 2005, she moved back in with Sandy and me at Hanson Lake. More news on the home front that year concerned my mother. She had enjoyed her Florida home for many years before the day came that she was diagnosed with Alzheimer's. The family made a decision to move her and her husband back to Maine. She had children in southern Maine, so we found a facility down there for her. To keep my last promise to my mother and oversee her needs, I filed for guardianship. According to Maine laws, that automatically goes to the spouse. It was a tense time that took preparation and persistence on my part, but the judge eventually awarded me co-guardianship.

The following year, Sandy and I decided to build our dream home a few miles away from where we had raised the kids. I had just turned 60 years old and figured it was now or never. We began construction on a perfect building spot that was bordered by cranberry and chokecherry trees. The acreage was abundant with wildflowers and birds, squirrels, deer, and butterflies. Behind the house were hills thick with fir and spruce, and plenty of birch and apple trees. A location like that meant I would need to build a new camp not far from the house, at a spot that overlooked a rolling countryside. A year later, we moved into what we knew would be our last home. I had hoped I was learning to cut back and relax. But I found it difficult.

Heidi and I were still running the Automatic Payroll franchise in Presque Isle. I had already made her a partner in the business by this time. I kept busy with community work and, among other things, was elected president of the Northern Maine Community College foundation board. I spearheaded a successful $3.5 million gifts campaign and put in place over the next three years, policies and procedures that would enable the foundation to grow. I got much gratification from such things, but no matter how much I piled onto my plate, I keep feeling something was missing. One morning in 2008, I realized that I had not been feeling up to par for some time. I went to one doctor's office after another, but none of them could determine what was ailing me.

I decided to try a well-known gastroenterologist, a liver specialist down in Portland. He diagnosed me with type 1 autoimmune hepatitis, a chronic disease that stimulates the immune system to attack the liver cells. The worst case scenarios, without proper treatment, are liver cancer and liver replacement. The doctor prescribed prednisone, the only treatment available at that time. In asking questions about the disease, we were told that it was most common in women ages 15 to 40.

It was a beautiful October day. On the drive home, Sandy tried to lift my spirits. "It's one way to get in touch with your feminine side, Ray," she said. That was probably the last light moment between us for some time when it came to autoimmune hepatitis. Sandy noticed a huge change in me when I'd been on the medication for less than a month, and it wasn't a positive one. I went from the mood swings she knew well to all-out rages. Anything and everything could set me off, no matter how trivial. I could explode in anger in seconds. We didn't realize what was happening, that prednisone raises the blood sugar level and mine was already high given my diabetes. The medication was wreaking havoc on my system. There was no rhyme and there was certainly no reason.

My whole life seemed to be spinning out of control and *beyond* my control, which had been my foremost fear. We visited our local church one day and began chatting with our priest. When I told him about my illness, he asked if he could give me the Rite of Anointing. According to the church's sacrament, and through the ministry of the priest, there is no need to wait until death is imminent to receive the Sacrament. If it's God's will, the person receiving it will be physically healed of illness. This anointing brought me a measure of peace.

But it was soon to get much worse. After a follow-up visit to the specialist in Portland, Sandy and I returned home early the following morning. It was in December, one of those below-zero-at-noon winter days so common to northern Maine. A light snow had fallen the day before and as we drove past the potato fields, they glistened beneath that fresh layer. When we turned into our drive leading up to the house, I said to Sandy, "I'm going to plow the drive before this snow turns to ice." I went to the garage where I kept my tractor and Sandy went inside the house to unpack our suitcases.

The tractor had a 60-inch scraper blade for plowing which attaches hydraulically. For safety measures I had always put wooden blocks on the floor under the blade when I attached it, just in case something went wrong. But it had been a long drive home from Bangor where we had spent the previous night. I had our visit with the specialist and my medical condition on my mind. Maybe that was the reason I opted not to use the blocks for the first time. The hydraulics let go and the blade—it weighed about 150 pounds— dropped on my left foot. Thankfully it bounced and I was able to pull my foot back before it dropped again. The pain was immediate and excruciating. I yelled for Sandy, but knew she wouldn't hear me. Walking on that foot was too painful, so I crawled to the house on my hands and knees, and into the mud room. When Sandy finally heard my shouts and opened the door, she thought I'd had a heart attack. "I just crushed my foot," I told her. "I need to go to the hospital."

The twenty-minute drive seemed to last forever. I was taken into the emergency room where my foot was examined. At noon, I was told I'd need surgery. When a life-threatening emergency came in, my foot had to wait. But it was a long wait. It was 7:30 that evening before I finally went into surgery. The doctor—it was luck that he was a visiting doctor from New York who specialized in crush injuries—put the damaged bones in my foot back together with metal plates and screws. Since I was already on prednisone, he prescribed an antibiotic plus oxycodone as a pain killer, and sent me home. "You'll be off your feet for six weeks," he told me. "But it will take longer than that to completely heal." It was as if a train that had been speeding ahead for years suddenly ran out of track. That's how I felt. I'd been nose to grindstone since I was a kid and this accident put the brakes on my constant running from whatever was pursuing me. There's no way to run if you can't even walk.

One evening, I insisted that we invite friends over for supper. Sandy was, of course, hesitant. But I persisted and so she made a very nice supper for us and our guests. Our friends had only just arrived when I decided Sandy should change the dressings on my foot. When that was done, I wanted her to find some papers I needed for work. Then I wanted phone numbers looked up for clients I should call the next day. Our polite guests, obviously sympathizing with Sandy, sat at our dining room table and ate alone. I apologized a lot in those days, Sandy told me.

I lay on the sofa for all those weeks, hobbling about as I could and trying to keep tabs on what Heidi was dealing with at the office. That daily dose of prednisone, now aided by oxycodone, pushed my blood sugar level so high that I don't know how Sandy remained with me. I know the kids kept their distance. If I had been difficult before, I was now impossible. When I finally got off the sofa and back on my feet, I returned to work. Two of my employees quit. Only Heidi, who had become like a daughter to me, weathered the storm. Sandy finally called the specialist in Portland and told him the prednisone wasn't working. He put me on azathioprine and things started calming back down. I felt normal again, but now I needed answers. Something was broken inside me and I knew it. I just couldn't give it a name.

The bad news kept on coming. I started forgetting where I'd put things, the names of people and places, or what events were on my schedule. I went in for a checkup and was diagnosed as possibly having the beginnings of Alzheimer's, or another form of dementia. Knowing that my mother had been diagnosed five years earlier and seeing firsthand what that meant, was devastating news. Since the tests were not conclusive, Sandy refused to accept it. "We need more information, Ray," she insisted. She went alone to the local agency on aging and talked to one of the counselors. What she learned was that many people are given this same diagnosis and incorrectly. We were referred to the Family Medical Institute in Augusta, our state capital. They were affiliated with Dartmouth College's Geisel School of Medicine and highly regarded. Sandy made an appointment for late August. When she came home and told me what she'd learned, I knew I couldn't give up. "Let's go to Augusta," I said.

It was a solemn drive south. During those four hours I ran over in my mind how I might handle my personal affairs if the earlier diagnosis was correct. This is what I'd done for my mother, after all, and she was in my thoughts that day. I would need to be certain that Sandy was in a position to carry on without me. I remembered what happened to my mother and our family when Dad died suddenly, and so young. I knew my wife was capable and smart enough to handle what came her way. Hell, she'd been handling *me* for years. But it would be best for us to sit down as a couple and make preparations for her future if the news was bad. As we were pulling into the clinic, Sandy said, "Ray, I just realized that today is August 28. It's been 48 years since your father died."

Maybe Hector Gauvin was looking out for me that day. After an intense evaluation I was diagnosed with Mild Cognitive Impairment, which is the stage between the expected decline of aging and the more serious decline of dementia. It was not the best news in the world, but at least it wasn't Alzheimer's.

Now Sandy and I were ready to continue looking for answers. What *was* the demon that had been racing behind me, bringing those mood swings, bringing the anger, the depression, the fears, and those awful dreams of soldiers crawling like zombies out of helicopters and walking toward me? We had heard of PTSD by then, of course. But if Sandy even broached the subject, I became agitated. I didn't want to talk to her or anyone else about Vietnam. I had chalked it up to a bad experience during wartime. I had spent that year at the mortuary, and now it was up to me to rise above it. It was my problem and no one else's. But it was now apparent that I couldn't fix it alone. Or I had been unable to do so since 1969, and God knows I'd tried. So, I went for counseling at the Veterans Administration in nearby Caribou. Finally, forty-one years after the plane lifted up over Saigon in June of 1969 and left the madness far below me, I had an answer. I was suffering from chronic severe Post-Traumatic Stress Disorder. Better known as PTSD. And my Mild Cognitive Disorder was a product of it.

It was only then that I told Sandy what I had been through in Vietnam. We had been married for almost 40 years, and I had never revealed the horrors of my military experience. I shook uncontrollably as I talked, and tears rolled down my cheeks. My mind was filled with dread. Would she still love me? Would she think I was a monster? Would she want to leave? Instead, tears began to roll down her cheeks as she listened in stunned silence. Finally, in the quiet way that I knew so well, she walked over and hugged me, saying, "How did you hold all this inside for almost 50 years? You went through hell and back over there, and you were bearing that burden all alone? It must have been horrible for you."

I began seeing a psychiatrist and even went to group counseling at the VA center.

Sandy went to sessions with other wives who had experienced what she was experiencing, women whose husbands had also been in the military during wartime and suffered from PTSD. It took six months before I could share with my therapist what I had done during my year with WDMET. I sat down one day before a blank sheet of paper and started writing as best I could what my job had required me to do.

I had been met at the helipad at Tan Son Nhut in early June, 1968, just before the monsoons began. I hadn't wanted to be in a war zone, but I was ready to bring my skills to my fellow soldiers. I would do my part and I hoped to avoid combat, which is why I had enlisted for three years. And then my commanding officer had taken me into the mortuary to explain WDMET's goals.

Given the number of young soldiers whose bodies passed beneath my X-ray box, and like the men across the hall from me in the mortuary itself, my PTSD was even worse than it would have been had I seen combat. Now I knew what had held me in its grip for years. Finally.

In 2010, I sold my last franchise of Advantage Payroll Services. The stress was just too much, and at 64 years old, I needed to reevaluate my future. The sale was for a substantial amount of money, enough that Sandy and I knew we could retire then and there if we wished. For many years I'd been involved with the Chamber of Commerce, the Jaycees, the Rotary Club, United Way, the March of Dimes, the Maine and National Association of Retarded Citizens, the Alcohol Information and Referral Service, and too many planning boards and councils to list. I knew I could quit any civic involvement too, and no one would fault me for it. The way I saw it, I had two choices. I could retire and disappear, or Sandy and I could find a new adventure.

In 2011, after living with Alzheimer's for six years, my mother finally passed away. I found comfort in knowing that she and I had made our peace long before and that I had done my best by her. That same year I was presented with the Lifetime Achievement

Award from our local Chamber of Commerce. It was gratifying to have my business colleagues and acquaintances recognize my community service. My mother would have been pleased to know this. She had appreciated the benefits of community firsthand when she found herself alone raising six children. A small army of people had stepped in back then to help us.

Not long after my mother's funeral, another important milestone occurred in my life. I was diagnosed with dyslexia. Now I understood what had been a lifelong stumbling block in school and later on in business. *This* was the reason I had to study harder than most of my classmates. It was the reason I'd carved the spelling of words, and math equations, and historic dates on the top of my bedroom desk back on Academy Street. Maybe it was also the reason that teacher told me I was stupid and would never amount to anything. Yet I had overcome the obstacle without knowing it existed. Better yet, I had more than proven that teacher wrong.

Instead of retirement, Sandy and I came up with a plan in 2012 called Aroostook Aspirations Initiative (AAI) that would expand our scholarship program. We had had monumental success with the Gauvin Family Scholarships, with 96 percent of our recipients finishing a college degree. We firmly believed that our mentoring of these students had played a major part in their successes. We felt the time had come to expand our program to include more students. Thus, AAI was born. We launched the program a year later, and in 2014 awarded our first scholarships. We also created mentoring and networking opportunities to give our scholars the tools necessary to succeed in college and also later in their careers. In essence, we take graduating high school seniors and follow them through the next four years. Even after they graduate college and leave the program, we are available as mentors if needed.

Our AAI training sessions, which our scholars attend each summer, come with a myriad of objectives. When they become college freshmen, they are introduced to the learning style that best suits them, whether visual, auditory, or tactile. We educate the college sophomores about "financial literacy," how to make, spend, and save their money, and even how to invest. We discuss ways to stay healthy and safe while in college, whether they live on or off campuses. We even hold dinners for them during which an expert teaches them table etiquette so they are prepared for business lunches and dinners. We arrange for speed interviews in which each student meets with local business owners to help prepare them for when the real job interview comes. Each year, we hold a Night with the Stars gala to celebrate our scholars as well as the businesses in Northern Maine who support us.

And, we aren't done there. The same year we launched AAI, our contributions to a local college, Northern Maine Community College, resulted in a technology wing being named for Sandy and me. I felt it honored my family's name. And it also paid tribute to Sandy's family, especially her late mother, Jackie Greaves, who was not just a school teacher herself but the first "counselor" I had when I first got back from Vietnam. Jackie had lured a troubled young soldier from off the porch steps and into her kitchen for a cup of coffee and positive conversation. The work that Sandy and I do together honors *both* of our families. As of this writing, we have had over 200 scholars graduate from our Aroostook Aspirations Initiative program and have given out approximately $310,000 through our scholarship programs. Our greatest wish is to impart a message that they will carry with them all their lives: "When, *not if,* you are successful, help the generations coming behind you so."

Learning that I have chronic PTSD doesn't mean that the stress has gone away, or the disturbing dreams have stopped. It just means that I now have a better way to cope. I use deep breathing techniques when I feel anxiety. I've learned to walk away from or completely avoid situations that may become stressful. On those husband-wife occasions when Sandy and I might disagree over something, I go to my shop and work on whatever project I've started. In the early years of our marriage, I'd stay mad for days. Now it lasts minutes. When I need alone time, I walk up to my camp

where I have privacy in the heart of nature's beauty. I still experience inexplicable sadness at times. And while I do take an antidepressant each day, what helps me even more are the positive mental attitude tapes I listen to, and the self-help books I read that deal with personal devel-

Ray enjoying his workshop

opment and spiritual wellness. No one said it would be easy. So each day I suit up.

If asked to choose, I would say that the best compliment I have ever received in my lifetime, the greatest accolade, came from my wife. The other day as we were talking about our most turbulent times over the years, Sandy smiled at me and said, "I never doubted you, Ray. All I had to do was remember the *real* you, and the many things that I love about you."

Epilogue

SOLDIER'S HEART—FULL CIRCLE

Τ he military uses certain words to describe the aftermath of wars, and what often befalls the soldiers who fight them. In the Civil War, soldiers coming home and suffering from depression were said to have *soldier's heart*. In World War I, it was *shell shock*. In World War II and Korea, it was *combat fatigue*. It took Vietnam and its aftermath for it to slowly turn into what it still is, *post-traumatic stress disorder*. And yet, only "soldier's heart" still reminds us of the human being who served his or her country. From there on, the words become clinical and detached. As with many of my fellow Vietnam veterans, I fought more than one war. There was my assignment in Saigon, and then there was the aftermath of Agent Orange and PTSD.

When one comes to analyzing the past in order to write a memoir, it's a lot like arranging those bones that lay on the tables back in Vietnam. What goes where? How does one connect the years of an entire life? The writer Thomas Wolfe says you can't go home again. That's because the past we knew as children is no longer there. But in the case of most soldiers coming home from a war, it's because the boy or man they were when they left no longer exists. That's how it was with me. I had to rebuild my life.

When the Internet came along and I could do research, I learned that WDMET *had* accomplished some good. We paved the way for Kevlar chest protectors, or vests, which even policemen wear today, not just the military. The vests and also helmets are much lighter now. Our Vietnam soldiers were taking off this protective equipment, because it was too heavy and too hot to wear in that tropical climate. Because of the great number of deaths that occurred from head wounds, we now have titanium helmets that are 10 times stronger than the old steel pot helmet worn in Vietnam, and 11 percent lighter. WDMET is still referred to in numerous medical papers, journals, and research projects. We are cited in ER, surgical, and wound treatment procedures that are now in place as standard practice. It helps for me to read things like this. And then, I was proud for having found a new X-ray technique for soft-tissue, multi-dimensional layers. I have to believe my year in Vietnam was worth something.

With our yearly scholarships going ahead, and our financial retirement secure, Sandy and I have come full circle as a couple. Our own two children are successful in their lives, which makes us proud. Nowadays, we enjoy traveling as often as we can, sometimes in the company of our spoiled and happy dogs, Bo, an English springer, and Tucker, a golden retriever. Seeing our children, and our scholars, go out into the world and do well for themselves has been both healing and heart-warming. But I still felt something was missing in my life. I guess it was that closure the talk show hosts refer to.

A major breakthrough in my healing process came when I decided to reconnect with my teammates at WDMET. In 1969, Colonel Ostrom had sent a dozen of his team members a Letter of Appreciation, myself included. So I had a short list of names to reference. Most were there the year before I was, so I didn't know them. But I searched for them all. I found obituaries for several. For half of the names, I found no information at all. I never found James W. Flowers. He had been my closest friend at Tan Son Nhut. Jim had even sent me a letter in 1999. He had been "kicking around

Missouri" once he retired from the army in 1983. He then became an adjunct professor of sociology and history at a private college in that state. I had obviously not been ready to stir up the old ghosts. I don't think I even wrote back. Over a decade passed before I did. By then, Jim Flowers's email and mailing addresses were no longer in use. Wherever he is, I wish him well.

I knew that the most important person for me to find would be Major Lane. When we started this book, I began a search online for him. He had been the chief pathologist on our team and a mentor to me. But 50 years is a long time. And then, all I could remember was his last name. He was always just Major Lane to me. A year passed and I had given up on the search. Then, early in 2018, my sister Diane, living in Florida, sent me a brown envelope filled with some of our mother's souvenirs that related to me.

The Christmas Card "Doc" Lane had sent Gladys and that, 50 years later, brought him and Ray back together

There were newspaper clippings from my early years, mentions of school and Boy Scout awards. She had also saved my letters from Vietnam. Among the letters and clippings I found an envelope dated December 1968. Inside was a beautiful Christmas card. *Chúa Mừng Giáng Sinh* was written on the front. That's the Christian way of saying *Merry Christmas* in Vietnamese. I opened the card and saw a few lines of handwriting.

> *Dear Mrs. Gauvin,*
>
> *I wish Ray could be spending the holiday season at home this year. He's doing a very commendable job for us. Best wishes,*
> *Major C. Darrell Lane, MC*

I was shocked to see his full name. And I was moved to know that he had been gracious enough to send cards to parents of the WDMET team members. My mother could never know the importance of saving that card, or how it would play a part in my healing process five decades later. That it reached me at all was miraculous considering it was mailed from Vietnam to northern Maine. It had gone with her to Florida when she moved down there. And it had been tucked away in storage for seven years after her death, until my sister mailed that packet to me. I call it fate.

Looking for a Major C. Darrell Lane raised the odds on my finding him. There was a phone listing in Pennsylvania for C. Darrell Lane. Was it the Major Lane I had known? And if it was, would he even remember me? I asked Sandy to make the initial phone call. Yes, he was the major who had served in the army at Tan Son Nhut in the late 1960s. Of course, he remembered Raynold Gauvin. It felt as if a big part of what I'd lost in Vietnam had returned. A brotherhood much deeper than friendship is formed among men who serve in the military together. Two days later, I called him myself. I could now talk to someone who didn't just know what I'd gone through, but who had gone through it with me. Sandy and I made plans to visit Major Lane and his wife.

Ray and Major Lane reunited in 2018, 50 years after they left Vietnam

On June 4, 2018, and almost 50 years to the day that I left Vietnam, Sandy and I flew to Pennsylvania. When Major Lane opened the door and smiled to see me, it was the smile I remembered. We sat over drinks and dinner, his family coming to meet Sandy and me. He told me much about WDMET and our time there that I didn't know. I had forgotten about the soldier killed by a tiger that Major Lane went on to write about for a military medical magazine. I had even forgotten the day I wrote about in this book, when the two girls on the scooter tried to kill us. That's how strong the human mind is in protecting a person's psyche from further damage. Being an experienced pathologist, and a decade older, Major Lane didn't experience PTSD as I and so many young soldiers would. His memory of our experience in Southeast Asia was vivid.

From Major Lane, I learned that the WDMET study was also conducted at Da Nang mortuary to the north by the Marines. Some of those studies were done on living soldiers. Major Lane had spent time up there, too. He was even asked to testify as an experienced pathologist at Lieutenant William Calley's trial over the My Lai massacre incident. He studied photographs to supply information on how victims had received certain wounds. He had come home to a long and successful career as a pathologist before retiring. Sandy and I visited Major Lane and his wife again—he will always be *Major Lane* to me—and we will now be in touch to the end. I am grateful for his friendship, and his continued guidance.

Many things have changed in 50 years. As would be expected, the two mortuaries in Vietnam were shut down when the war ended. After Saigon fell, Tan Son Nhut Air Base was seized and became a facility for the Vietnam People's Air Force, which it remains today. The country itself, the flora and fauna, have rebounded. But warfare always leaves its indelible marks. I know some of my fellow veterans have returned to Vietnam since the war ended, and I applaud them for that. But it's not a goal of mine. My future is here. Our first grandchild, a boy named Jimmy, was born in the summer of 2019. What more can Sandy and I ask for? A new generation will take up the reins and carry the torch forward. We hope the world will be a safe place for them.

With Sandy at my side—the girl who still loads her arms down with books—I guess I'm more than a survivor. I'm a damn lucky man. These days, as I face the future with her beside me, I choose to think that what I deal with on a daily basis is *soldier's heart*. It reminds me that I was, indeed, a soldier once. And knowing this fills me with me pride.

Ray and Sandy, October, 2020

Acknowledgements

To all of those who died during the Vietnam War, and those veterans who have returned and experienced the effects of PTSD and Agent Orange. To those veterans who have suffered the ravages of war and, upon coming home, have faced the challenge of holding together a marriage and a family. And to those veterans who find themselves homeless, with no family. Thank you all for your sacrifice. You have paid a great price for your service. It is my hope that you can find at least peace, if not happiness.

I want to thank the following people for their contribution to the development of *A Soldier's Heart*: Bill Streepy, Susan Bailey, Scott Smith, Sandy Gauvin, Major C. Darrell Lane, Diane Parent, Peter Macomber, Jr., Diana Tilley, Gilman Gauvin, Delcia Goode, Gary Gauvin, Gary Redlinski, Adrian Gagnon, and Dr. Jim Page. They all provided important pieces of information that have gone into the book.

I am grateful to the following people for their review and sensitive comments about the manuscript: Sandy Gauvin, Martin Harband, Susan Bailey, Scott Smith, Diane Parent, Bill Honaker, Col. Judy Carroll, Don Tardie, MAJ C. Darrell Lane, Greg LaFracois, Dr. Sarah Bushey, Bill McCloud, Brett Emblin, and other friends. They contributed greatly to the dialogue and made valuable suggestions about the manuscript.

Thanks to Laura Cutler, archivist of The National Museum of Health and Medicine, for helping us find the research files for WDMET and directing us in how to view the files.

Thanks to John Stephenson for the photo of the Welcome to Vietnam sign he had taken in Jan., 1968 (p.104). He had posted it on hamptonroadsnavalmuseum.blogspot.com

I also want to thank Jim Flowers, who wrote to me in January of 1999 to enlist my help in finding other members of our team. I regret to this day that I did not respond to his letter due to my fear of bringing back terrible memories. It wasn't until 2014 that I started contemplating the idea of writing a book about my experience. I decided to contact Jim for help. Unfortunately, I was not able to find him. It was his letter that started the ball rolling and gave me enough courage to talk about my experiences.

Thank you to all those veterans that brought me out of the darkness during those many therapy sessions we shared. It was their honesty and willingness to tell their stories that gave me the courage to tell mine.

I would especially like to acknowledge my commander in Vietnam, Major C. Darrell Lane, with whom I was recently able to reconnect. Our reunion came about as the result of a simple act of kindness performed 50 years ago. His friendship and counsel have finally ended my survivor's guilt and restored my self-respect.

Thank you to Theresa Mosher of Mosher Multi-Media in Presque Isle, Maine, for her contribution to the development of the Aroostook County and Viet Nam maps.

And a special thank you to John Lisnik, for his observations, his help, and his support in recognizing (and helping me recognize) my PTSD. May you rest in peace, John.

Thank you to all my family, relatives, and friends who were subjected to my PTSD demons. Those were difficult times for me, and my behaviors were not always easy to deal with. I was overcome by feelings of shame, guilt, and loss of self-respect, and I masked them with anger and impatience. I did not even recognize my negative actions. You didn't give up on me, and for that, I will be eternally grateful.

And last of all, I would like to acknowledge the living and deceased members of the WDMET team who served alongside me: CPT Michael Leaken, CPT George H. Ishler, MSG Samson O. Lee, SSG Fred C. Hall, Jr., SSG Ronald Spurgeon, SSG Thomas S. Straub, SSG Raynold L. Eaton, SP5 James W. Flowers, COL Thomas Ostrom, and Major Charles Darrell Lane. The work we did together was not easy, but it was significant. I hope you have been able to find peace and happiness as you have moved forward.

For me, writing this book has opened the door to the vulnerability of letting people into my innermost secrets. But I believe the risk was worth it if I could help one veteran deal with the ravages of war and its after-effects. It can take control over the veteran's physical, mental, emotional, and spiritual well-being, as well as that of those around them. It is my hope that this book will let that veteran understand that he is not alone and he should not wait as long as I did to get help.

About the Author

Ray Gauvin is a Vietnam Veteran and prominent business and community leader in the State of Maine. He has a Bachelor's degree in Accounting and Business Management. Born to a blended Canadian and American family of Acadian descent, Ray grew up navigating between speaking French at home and English at school. He would learn later in life that he had also been battling with dyslexia. While in the army, he received the Army Commendation Medal and was recommended to receive the Bronze Star. Having lost his father at a young age, Gauvin discovered early that he had a talent for entrepreneurship. In 1984, he started the Center for Financial Planning and popularized the concept of financial planning in northern Maine. At one time, Gauvin owned franchises of Advantage Payroll Services in four New England states. He and his wife Sandy created the Gauvin Lighthouse Fund and the Gauvin Family Scholarship. Currently, they are co-founders of the Aroostook Aspirations Foundation, a nonprofit that helps first-generation students complete a college education and move into a successful career. They have two children and a grandson and live in northern Maine with their two dogs, Bo and Tucker.

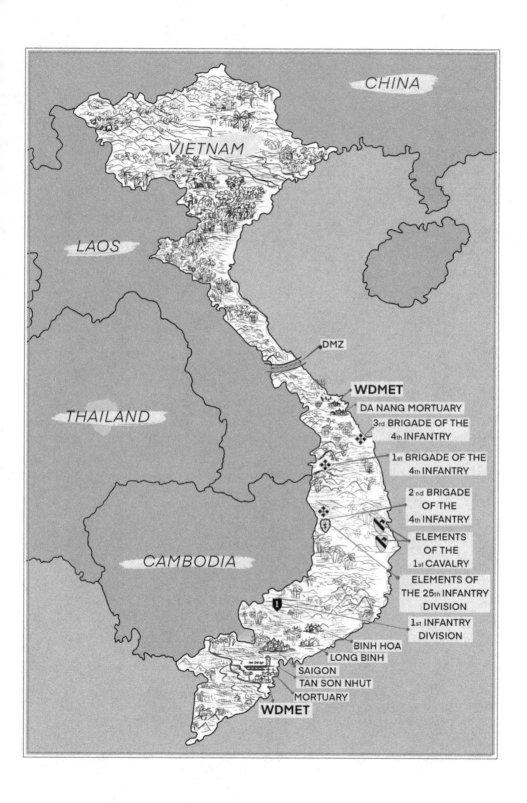

CPSIA information can be obtained
at www.ICGtesting.com
Printed in the USA
BVHW031652140922
647052BV00015B/517

9 781039 100930